The Spirit Filled Home

A Study of the Biblical Basis for a Joy Filled Home and Family

M J Tiry

The Spirit Filled Home

By M. J. Tiry

"[11] For what man knoweth the things of a man, save the spirit of man which is in him? even so the things of God knoweth no man, but the Spirit of God. [12] Now we have received, not the spirit of the world, but the spirit which is of God; that we might know the things that are freely given to us of God. [13] Which things also we speak, not in the words which man›s wisdom teacheth, but which the Holy Ghost teacheth; comparing spiritual things with spiritual. [14] But the natural man receiveth not the things of the Spirit of God: for they are foolishness unto him: neither can he know *them*, because they are spiritually discerned. [15] But he that is spiritual judgeth all things, yet he himself is judged of no man. [16] For who hath known the mind of the Lord, that he may instruct him? But we have the mind of Christ." (1Cor. 2:11-16)

The Spirit Filled Home

A Study of the Spiritual Resources Available for a Functional Marriage, Family and Home Life

Author: M J Tiry

Published March 2026 by M J Tiry Publishing

All Scripture References in this book are taken from the King James Version of the Bible.

The Spirit Filled Home / M J Tiry

ISBN: 979-8-9918240-5-7 Paper

ISBN: 979-8-9918240-6-4 Hard Cover

ISBN: 979-8-9918240-7-1 eBook

Library of Congress Control Number: 2026906528

Print Information Available on the Last Page

TABLE OF CONTENTS

PREFACE

Many years ago I had fallen in love with a message in the Word of God. That message has put joy in my heart. I share that joy with the apostle Paul as he says in Acts 20:24 "But none of these things move me, neither count I my life dear unto myself, so that I might finish my course with joy, and the ministry, which I have received of the Lord Jesus, to testify the gospel of the grace of God." That joy continues to this day as I minister the riches of God's grace to men and women (and boys and girls) the life giving, the life saving, transforming work of the Holy Spirit as He ministers the "Word of his grace which is able to build you up, and to give you an inheritance amoung all them that are sanctified." (Acts 20:32)

I have been ministering the riches of God's grace to people in one way or another for nearly fifty years. That ministry involved not only teaching and preaching the gospel of grace but counseling with people in their homes on marriage and family issues. Unfortunately, it often involved helping people pick up the pieces of shattered lives and putting the pieces of dysfunctional homes and broken lives back together. In it all, I thank God that His grace is not about hanging people with mistakes of the past. Rather, it is about rebuilding and restoring lives that have been wrecked by the three-fold enemy of the world, the flesh and the devil. I have to say, that three-fold enemy has been effective in undermining our culture and society here in America.

As I look at society at large and consider the state of homes and family life, it is apparent that there is danger that all is in grave danger of decline in America. There is, however, much cause for optimism because there is still a strong marriage and family ethos in America. I surmise that there are three reasons for the health of the institutions of marriage and family wherever I find it as being from three sources -- those being 1) nature, 2) nurture, and 3) scripture. There are some folks who have a good nature that seems to predispose them to function well in marriage and family. Then there are folks who grew up in stable homes in which the institution of marriage and family were greatly valued, properly modeled, and internalized to be a part of the very fabric of their social interactions. Finally, there are some folk who did not have the benefit of the first two sources and have thus failed in marriage and family life yet have found in the scripture the resources to find success in spite of the lack of seeing it modeled themselves in their home background. It is toward the success of this last group that I particularly direct this study in the Word of God.

ACKNOWLEDGEMENTS

About the Cover: The cover is a painting by my daughter Naomi Tiry Salgado. Pictured in the painting are three of my granddaughters Miranda, Ashlyn, and Sofie. The painting is based on a photo taken at my youngest daughter's wedding.

In Appreciation: I appreciate the work of Vince Kison, Rochelle McQuellen, my daughter Naomi Tiry Salgado and my wife Linda Tiry for their work in reviewing this document. I thank my daughter Anna Tiry Anderson for her work in design of the cover and formatting. I also thank my daughter Naomi for her work in the publishing process.

Note to the reader: In several chapters an expository presentation of the passage of scripture is presented. For example, you will find an expository study of Romans Chapters 6, 7, and 8 in Chapter 4 of this book. Follow the annotation note [a] to the annotations below the passage designated [a] for an in depth study of that portion of the passage.

References Cited:

Abbreviations used:

c.	circa ("about/Approximately")
cp	Compare
e.g.	exampligratia ("for example")
et. al.	Et allii ("and others")
etc.	Et. cetara ("and so forth")
ff	and the following (verses, pages, etc.)
i.e.	id. est. (that is)
vs, vv	verse (s)
viz.	Videlicet ('namely")

INTRODUCTION

The *Spirit Filled Home* – is the title of this book. The theme of this book is the Christian home being filled with the work of the Holy Spirit of God. Being thus filled, the blessed work of the Spirit of God is manifest in the life of each person in that home. What a lofty goal that is! Yet such a goal is achievable. Reaching that goal is possible because it is the work of God in the lives of people who simply make decisions based upon information found in the Word of God. The most fundamental decision is to personally choose to trust in the redeeming work that the Lord Jesus Christ did on our behalf on Calvary. The spiritual resources by which anyone can live a victorious life here on planet earth are available to everyone as a result of His soul saving, redeeming work. We just appropriate those resources by faith and then (by faith) we apply them. As the believer trusts in that redeeming work of Jesus Christ, the Holy Spirit goes to work in that person's life to equip the soul to live life on the high plane of being a child of God.

"11 For what man knoweth the things of a man, save the spirit of man which is in him? even so the things of God knoweth no man, but the Spirit of God. 12 Now we have received, not the spirit of the world, but the spirit which is of God; that we might know the things that are freely given to us of God. 13 Which things also we speak, not in the words which man's wisdom teacheth, but which the Holy Ghost teacheth; comparing spiritual things with spiritual. 14 But the natural man receiveth not the things of the Spirit of God: for they are foolishness unto him: neither can he know them, because they are spiritually discerned. 15 But he that is spiritual judgeth all things, yet he himself is judged of no man. 16 For who hath known the mind of the Lord, that he may instruct him? But we have the mind of Christ." (1Corinthians 2:11-16)

We note that the term "spirit which is of God..." in Verse 12 is in the lower case "s." This is talking about the human spirit that is tuned into the Spirit of God – the Holy Ghost. This passage is talking about the Holy Ghost teaching spiritual things (spiritual concepts) to people whose human spirits have been regenerated by the work of the Holy Spirit of God. Regeneration is the process by which the Holy Spirit imparts life to the human spirit of the natural man. Once that happens, that individual is no longer a "natural man" – he or she is no longer the same in his spiritual makeup from what he was when he was born into the world. We understand from this passage that the natural man is not only unable to receive the things of the Spirit of God but he is not able to "know" them because his spirit is not in a condition to acquire such knowledge. However, "he that is spiritual..." is a person who went through a process of spiritual transformation that the Bible calls "Regeneration" and then went further on in a study of scripture so as to learn to live as a son of God. Regeneration is the work that the Holy Spirit does in, and on behalf of the person who has trusted the Lord Jesus Christ as Savior. Titus 3:5 talks about that saying

Titus 3:5-7 "5 Not by works of righteousness which we have done, but according to his mercy he saved us, by the washing of regeneration, and renewing of the Holy Ghost; 6 Which he shed on us abundantly through Jesus Christ our Saviour; 7 That being justified by his grace, we should be made heirs according to the hope of eternal life."

This study will look at the work that the Holy Spirit does in the believer as the believer walks by faith in the marvelous work of grace that God does in the lives of members of the body of Christ in this present Dispensation of Grace. The Holy Spirit does eight things in and for the believer at the instant of conversion (at the instant of soul salvation by personal faith that Jesus Christ fully paid sin's debt in full for the believer and that soul thus receives the gift of eternal life). We will look at these works in more detail later but for now we just list them. Everything that God will do in the believer's life after the initial regeneration all go back to these eight things that were done on the believer's behalf when he or she first trusted Jesus Christ as Savior.

The works of the Holy Spirit of God are:

1. He **Baptizes** the believer into an eternal spiritual union with our Lord Jesus Christ (1Cor. 12:12-13; Rom. 6:3; Gal. 3:27). This baptism has nothing to do with water but it has everything to do with the believer being totally and eternally identified with the Savior in His redeeming work on our behalf on Calvary.

2. He **Circumcises** with a spiritual circumcision (Phil. 3:3; Col. 2:11; 3:11). This is a work that effects a spiritual separation of the outward man that perishes (the physical body) from the inward man (the soul and spirit) that is renewed day by day (2Cor. 4:16).

3. He **Regenerates** the believer's human spirit by imparting spiritual life to it (Titus 3:5). This work is what gives the believer the capacity to begin to understand the things of God that are revealed in the Word of God.

4. He **Takes up Residence** within the very physical body of the believer (1Cor. 6:19; Rom. 8:11).

5. He **Seals** the believer to eternal life (Eph. 1:13; 1Cor. 1:22; 2Cor. 5:5). This sealing work makes the believer's soul salvation secure in Christ.

6. He **Washes** the believer (1Cor. 6:11). This washing cleanses the believer of the stain of sin and equips the believer to stand before God. It was the cleansing blood of Christ that did this cleansing (Rev. 1:5). This cleansing enables God to make the believer "accepted in the beloved." (Eph. 1:3)

7. He **Sanctifies** us (1Cor. 6:11). This made each believer God's unique possession. This sanctification makes the believer a saint.

8. He **Justifies** each believer (1Cor. 6:11; Rom. 3:24-28; 4:5; 5:1; 5:9; 8:30). This is the act of God to impute the righteousness of Jesus Christ to the believer's account (2Cor. 5:21)

That wonderful work of God becomes the spiritual resource that every member of the Body of Christ (the church of this present Dispensation of Grace) can tap into by faith to appropriate spiritual victories in life. The believer can thus truly "reign in life by Jesus Christ" (Rom. 5:17-18). It is the author's hope and desire that the reader can see, understand, and apply these operating principles of the Holy Spirit laid out in this study. I prayerfully beseech you the reader to study these principles over an open Bible and then apply them by faith. The joy of having a spirit filled home awaits you.

CHAPTER 1
GODLINESS IS BIBLE BASED
CHARACTER PUT INTO ACTION

Godliness as a Goal

"When I was a child, I spake as a child, I understood as a child, I thought as a child: but when I became a man, I put away childish things." (1Corinthians 13:11)

The fact of the matter is that all of us who are parents were once children – but we grew up. We can therefore relate to all that children go through in the process of growing up. As parents we certainly ought to have a sense of awe as these precious lives come into our homes. We dads especially have an awakening when that precious new life was first placed into our hands. It was at that moment that it fully dawns on us what was happening as our wives went through pregnancy and delivery. We were there largely as observers but she was truly into it 100%. I recall when our first child was placed into my arms and I marveled at the awesomeness of it all. Here is a totally self contained living human being that did not exist until she was conceived some nine months earlier. There was no extension cord connected to her, no input screen, no keyboard, just this prettiest little package here in my arms and ready for whatever lies ahead for her in life – and there was no instruction manual that came with her. What struck me after I marveled at the experience of it all was the reality that eighteen years from now this child who just entered my home will begin the process of exiting it. How well equipped she will be for life will be largely in my hands and those of my wife as our responsibility.

Questions came to mind as I pondered all of that. What will be her character? What will be the value system on which she will base her decisions in life? On what principles will she operate as she lives her life here on planet earth? And then the question that really got me to thinking -- Where will she spend eternity and how will she be enjoying it? Actually these were questions that my wife and I addressed for ourselves not all that long before. Both of us came to saving knowledge of Christ later in life in our mid to late twenties. How thankful we were that we had something so precious as eternal life to share with this child and with any other that would follow her into our lives and become a part of our home. I realized then that, what I was hoping to share with our children, is what the Bible calls godliness.

Godliness is in essence the mental and spiritual preparation for the Christian life and, indeed, for parenting. There is a Bible passage that talks about godliness being a mystery. The passage is 1Timothy 3:16 – "And without controversy great is the mystery of godliness: God was manifest in the flesh, justified in the Spirit, seen of angels, preached unto the Gentiles, believed on in the world, received up into glory." The passage calls godliness a mystery but there is nothing mysterious about it. Godliness in that passage is simply God being manifest in the flesh (in the very lives) of believers. My first impression of this verse is that it is talking about our Lord as God manifest in the flesh as John 1:14 states: "...And the Word was made flesh, and dwelt among us..." The passage is actually talking about God being manifest in the flesh of believers. That is the concept of God indwelling believers as Romans 8:9-11 and Galatians 3:16 indicate. He does that indwelling as a result of a person being regenerated by personal faith in the redeeming work of our Lord Jesus Christ on Calvary. Yet godliness is more than that. It is God's character and personality being manifest in our lives. It is the very life of Christ being lived out in our lives. Galatians 2:20 says it well: "Christ liveth in me and the life that I now live in the flesh, I live by the Son of God who loved me and gave himself for me..."

It occurs to me as I observe God at work in the lives of believers and in family life that godliness is more caught than taught. You get what you model more than what you teach (or demand). Therefore, step one in successful parenting is to model godliness in one's personal life. Just as physical conditioning requires physical exercise, godliness (spiritual conditioning) requires spiritual exercise.

> But refuse profane and old wives' fables, and exercise thyself rather unto godliness. For bodily exercise profiteth little: but godliness is profitable unto all things, having promise of the life that now is, and of that which is to come. (I Timothy 4:7-8)

Exercise thyself unto Godliness

To exercise oneself unto godliness requires being filled with the Spirit. We will be studying passages that speak of being filled with the Spirit. We want to consider the possibility of having a Spirit filled home. Obviously, having a Spirit filled home requires the presence of Spirit filled parents. But how do parents become filled with the Spirit? We can understand how this is possible by comparing two passages that talk about the results of being filled with the Spirit. I direct your attention to the two passages below:

> "And be not drunk with wine, wherein is excess; but be filled with the Spirit; Speaking to yourselves in psalms and hymns and spiritual songs, singing and making melody in your heart to the Lord; Giving thanks always for all things unto God and the Father in the name of our Lord Jesus Christ;..." (Ephesians 5:18-20)

> "Let the word of Christ dwell in you richly in all wisdom; teaching and admonishing one another in psalms and hymns and spiritual songs, singing with grace in your hearts to the Lord. And whatsoever ye do in word or deed, do all in the name of the Lord Jesus, giving thanks to God and the Father by him." (Colossians 3:16-17)

We see from the Ephesians passage that being filled with the Spirit results in "Speaking to yourselves in psalms and hymns and spiritual songs, singing and making melody in your heart to the Lord..." while in the Colossians passage it is letting the Word of Christ dwell in you richly that does the same thing. So how then is one filled with the Spirit? It is by letting the word of Christ dwell in you richly. That is; to saturate your human spirit with the Word of God so that it literally dwells in you so as to feel at home in you and you feeling at home in the Word. This takes a continual study of the Word. This involves yielding oneself to the Word, and then living it out in life. Romans 6:13-14 addresses such yielding saying "[13] Neither yield ye your members *as* instruments of unrighteousness unto sin: but yield yourselves unto God, as those that are alive from the dead, and your members *as* instruments of righteousness unto God. [14] For sin shall not have dominion over you: for ye are not under the law, but under grace." This speaks of two different powerful influences in the believer's life – that being the indwelling sin nature and the other being the Spirit of God. In Verse 13 we see the word yield used twice. The first use is in the present tense indicating that this yielding to the sin nature is action that the believer can be doing continually. The second use of yield is in the aorist tense (in the Greek grammar) indicating that this is actually a decision that the believer makes that is a once for all decision whereby the believers resolves to appropriate the victory over sin that was won for him by the work of Jesus Christ on the cross. While Chapter 3 of Romans presents the doctrine of deliverance from the penalty of sin, Chapter 6 teaches the believer of his deliverance from the power of the sin nature to destroy lives. This is the power of the working of the grace of God to make a positive change in lives of believers. We will pick up on this thought more in later chapters.

There is yet another verse on godliness that we need to consider. There is a true godliness that is profitable for not only this life but also for the life to come but there is a false form of godliness that must be avoided with regard to family life because children can spot it quickly. Paul talks about it in 2Timothy 3:5: "Having a form of godliness, but denying the power thereof: from such turn away."

The full text reads: "This know also, that in the last days perilous times shall come. For men shall be lovers of their own selves, covetous, boasters, proud, blasphemers, disobedient to parents, unthankful, unholy, Without natural affection, trucebreakers, false accusers, incontinent, fierce, despisers of those that are good, Traitors, heady, highminded, lovers of pleasures more than lovers of God; Having a form of godliness, but denying the power thereof: from such turn away." (2Timothy 3:1-5) This reference to the last days of this present Dispensation of Grace in which perilous times shall come is talking about the days in which we live today. We will consider this false godliness more in Chapter 5 "Dealing with Life in the 21st Century."

True godliness has the power to transform life but false godliness does not. Paul talks about this in the passages (2Tim. 3:1-4) that precede our text passage. He is talking about the perilous times that shall come – which times we are in now in the twenty - first century. Note that the passage says that "men shall be..." without distinguishing between saved and unsaved men. We are in those perilous times when even some believers are involved in a form of godliness that does not have the power to change lives because it is not Bible based. True godliness stems from a steady diet of expository teaching of the Word of God. We will see more on this later in Chapter 5.

The Spirit Filled Home

The components of a Spirit filled home include: a father, a mother, a marriage, and children – but those are what is needed for a home. The Spirit filled home has to have all of that with the active presence of the Holy Spirit added to it. The Holy Spirit enters the home life through faith of the individuals who comprise the home. It might be just one member of the family that becomes a believer. Though this does not make the entire home Spirit filled, it enables the Holy Spirit to be actively at work in the home through that one member. The ideal is that every home be a Christian home and that every member of each Christian home be Spirit filled. What a wonderful world we would live in if that were the case!

But, not every home will meet this ideal – this is not a perfect world and we are not perfect people. Doubtless all homes will come short of the ideal in one or more ways. Yet, God is at work in the world of the imperfect. We do have a perfect Savior who will meet people where ever they are at in their particular level of spiritual maturity and functionality. God is after all in the business of getting lost people saved and conforming believers to the image of His Son (Romans 8:28-29). In fact, He is in the business of taking lives that have been wrecked by sin and making something beautiful of those lives. He is in the life changing business.

Super-abounding Grace

Romans 5:20 says "Where sin abounded, grace did much more abound." What has wreaked havoc in our world is sin but there is something that can and will defeat sin. That is the grace of God. Law, law keeping, and religious observances can not do it. We are talking about the prospect of our homes being Spirit filled homes but we need to start with a consideration of what is the basic fact of life in every home – whether they are believers or not. Not to throw or cast disparaging words into anyone's self image, but it is a fact of life that every dad has a sin nature and so does every mother and so does every child that is born of them. There was only one child born into the human race who did not have a sin nature. That child had a human mother but did not have a human father. We understand therefore that the sin nature is passed on through the male line. As a believing father of five children, I am glad that I have the knowledge of where sin comes from and how it works in the human race because I now know how I can teach my children that they can have the victory over it. We will study how to have that victory in Chapter 4.

This study could have been called "Grace Parenting" because grace is the means whereby God defeats sin. "Moreover the law entered, that the offense might abound. But where sin abounded, grace did much more abound: That as sin hath reigned unto death, even so might grace reign through righteousness unto eternal life by Jesus Christ our Lord." (Romans 5:20-21). What moves people from being servants of sin to reigning in life is a form of doctrine. We will talk more on that form of doctrine later but we leave the subject for now with this verse from Romans 6 "But God be thanked, that ye were the servants of sin, but ye have obeyed from the heart that form of doctrine which was delivered you." (Romans 6:17) We consider also the verse from Romans 5, "For if by one man's offense death reigned by one; much more they which receive abundance of grace and of the gift of righteousness shall reign in life by one, Jesus Christ." (Romans 5:17). We understand then that it is possible to reign in life by Jesus Christ. More on this later but now let's consider what children need in order to grow and develop to be godly citizens of earth and to grow so as to eventually do and be what God would have them be as citizens of heaven. We as believers have a duel citizenship. We live on planet earth but we do so as citizens of heaven (Philippians 3:20).

What we as parents need in order to provide for Children a fully functional home life: Entertainment Needs

For us as adults, productive activity is a primary focus in life while recreation activity is secondary. Small children however, live to play. It is as Paul said in 1Corinthians 13:11, "When I was a child, I thought as a child..." Children would not work if not constrained to do so. Yet in the process of maturing, children grow from basically full time play to full time work as they move into adulthood. In a span of 14 plus years, they grow from toys strewn across the floor to an array of competitive sporting activities, creative hobbies, developing talents in music, art, games, and such like activities. That which parents regard as good healthy activities on the part of pre-teens and teens can be a challenge to keep up with. Their fast changing interests, high level of energy, and youthful enthusiasm can be exhausting.

Kids love the thrill of simple things like tubing on snow, skating on ice, or moving fast in anything on wheels.

Then, as they graduate beyond those simple things, the more exhilarating experiences like mastering roller skates, skate boards, and surfing to the more high tech stuff of the digital world – which, in these days, they seem to master with the same ease as learning speech.

Play is an important part of the growing up process. It is the never ending thrill of achievement that ultimately produces real life skills that constitutes an adult ready for life. It started with the ten month old discovering the freedom of learning to crawl to the ten year old climbing to the top of trees to the 18 year old learning hang gliding. To us as parents (and grandparents) we realize that it is dangerous being a kid. Yet it is through this growth that he or she gains life skills and the confidence that they can master what life has to offer them. The most profit that can be gained from such play is gained when mom and dad join in the play – especially if there might be some element of danger in it. Even when danger is not a factor, it is important for children to know that mom and/or dad are there (whether you are physically involved or just carefully watching from a distance).

The parent - child relationship from such involvement in their play will last them and you a lifetime. We as parents do need to divert as much of our time as we can from the mundane affairs of life to engage them in their play. Engaging in activities as hunting, fishing, archery, playing ball and the like will not only form memories, but provide the format to teach safety in these potentially risky ventures.

Social Life

While play is essentially a full time endeavor for the young child, social engagement with others becomes the primary activity as they move into the mid-teen years. We as parents need to realize that our children's social engagements have the potential to impact them positively. We also understand that the impact can be negative. Therefore careful consideration of discerning parents is needed in providing guidance regarding social engagements.

In today's world, the opportunities for social engagement abound. There is today a vast array of social media available and easy to access. They are easy to join and are in fact specifically designed to appeal to young people. There are parents that I know of who join social media simply to stay abreast of what their children are involved in and to actually communicate with them.

As kids move into the mid-teen years, another powerful influence comes into play in their frame of reference. It is called puberty. When God created man as free moral agents, He did it so as to create a human race that can reproduce more of the same free moral agents. In doing so, He put into man's makeup a drive that would ensure success in reproduction – the sex drive. It is by divine design that the sexual drive constitutes the most controlling temptation a boy (or a man) will deal with. It is only the strength of character and the moral and ethical moral bedrock established in younger years that gives young men the self control to navigate through those emotionally troubling years into functional adulthood.

Girls on the other hand, are not initially in possession of such as powerful a drive but they do have a God given desire to be loved and treasured by a man. This does render them especially vulnerable to the predatory schemes of immoral males. Girls can easily become taken in and even addicted to male attention. Girls in unhappy homes are particularly vulnerable to "jumping ship" and fall into the first male arms that seem to be available to them.

Considering the delicate state of young people in teen years and young people in general, we wonder what resources are needed to enable them to stay the course to a fulfilling and godly family life down the road. Ideally, it is the strength of character that comes from the Holy Spirit of God working in their lives through the Word of God that will give them that. There is a spiritual fortitude that is built into a young person's life flowing from the nurturing of godly parents in a godly home. However, the real strength of character will be from decisions that young people make in the "inner man." (Eph. 3:17)

As concerned parents we tend to insulate our children from such vulnerability to the negative influences in life by sheltering them from it. That works only for a short time. We start garden plants in greenhouses to give them vigor to stand the competition and the harsher environment of the garden. However, we do eventually put them in the environment that they were raised to be in. So too it is an exercise in futility to totally isolate kids from the world. You can not isolate them from their own imaginations or their passions. They do simply need to understand their own passions and to understand what sin (the sin nature) is and what spiritual resources they have been provided by the Word of God, the Holy Spirit, and their life in Christ to equip them to deal with it and to not yield to sin.

Young people will formulate in their minds the ideal mate from impressions from their home life, from the community they associate with, and from the world around them. The way of wisdom, however is to temper all of that input by information gleaned from the Word of God.

We are instructed as dads not to provoke our children to wrath but to bring them up in the nurture and admonition of the Lord (Eph. 6:4). External control of a person when it overrides the internal motivation of the heart produces wrath. When the time is right, the external control has to be released so that the spirit within the child can express itself, being in tune with the Spirit of God working through the Word of God. This involves a dad (and mom) who are filled with the Spirit themselves providing nurturing that will eventually lead to Spirit filled children, who in turn become Spirit filled parents in their own right, leading their own Spirit filled homes. Providing for a social life for young people involves a delicate balance between a controlled, supervised social life and wisdom directed maturity in their hearts. We want to provide loving guidance to our children so that they become our equal in maturity (and in son-ship as sons of God). We want to see a heart anchored in the Word of God with the potential to even surpass us in stature both personally and spiritually as they advance in the Word. To exercise too much control is to provoke wrath in our children. We do not like being under someone's control so as to have a lack of autonomy. Our children do not like it either. We want them to be their own person making their own wise decisions in life. Parenting is therefore a gradient from complete control at birth to full fellowship among peers in adulthood. We will look at the matter of when and how to let go in Chapter 3.

Children need Grace: Where sin abounded, Grace did much more abound

We ask ourselves, what will give young people the spiritual, moral, and ethical maturity to be properly adjusted to the indwelling sin nature? For a quick answer, it is the grace message properly understood and applied that gives young people (and indeed all saints) the spiritual wherewithal to gain victory over sin (that being the sin nature that resides in every member of our human race). "Moreover the law entered, that the offence might abound." For a more detailed answer, it is an understanding of the work of the Holy Spirit that gives the victory over sin. "But where sin abounded grace did much more abound…" (Romans 5:20). The message that our Lord revealed through Paul the apostle of the gospel of the grace of God provides for us that which the law demanded of us but which the law could not produce in us (Romans 8:1-4). What the law could not do (instilling righteous conduct and godly living), grace did. Grace can actually produce the righteous standard of conduct that the Law demanded of those who were under it but could not produce in their lives because the Law (as does all external motivation) depended on the flesh. Our primary goal then as parents is to introduce our children to the doctrine of grace and to demonstrate grace in action in our lives so as to model grace in action for them.

The body of doctrine that encompasses the Pauline revelation is called "the mystery" because it was kept secret until the time was right to reveal it. When the time was right, Our Lord revealed it through the apostle Paul. It is a doctrine that is totally intertwined with the working of the Holy Spirit in the lives of believers today in the Dispensation of Grace. It is all the outworking of the Holy Spirit who indwells the believer the moment that the sinner makes his or her decision to trust 100% in the redeeming work of Jesus Christ on Calvary. We will address that in more detail in Chapter 4.

Children need to see how the grace of God works. Grace stands in contrast to Law and the Law principle. The message of Romans Chapter 8 is that grace can and will produce in the lives of believers the righteous conduct that law demanded but could not produce. Paul says: "[15] Because the law worketh wrath: for where no law is, *there is* no transgression. [16] Therefore *it is* of faith, that *it might be* by grace; to the end the promise might be sure to all the seed; not to that only which is of the law, but to that also which is of the faith of Abraham; who is the father of us all…" (Romans 4:15-16) Paul also instructs fathers: "[4] And, ye fathers, provoke not your children to wrath: but bring them up in the nurture and admonition of the Lord." (Ephesians 6:4) God deals with us on the basis of grace. Fathers need to understand how grace works and to learn to apply it in parenting.

Children need Truth

Certainly one of the greatest skills that children need is to find and take hold of truth. Children need to see truth honored and venerated so as to truly appreciate its value. They need to know that absolute truth is available to them. However that truth can only be found in one person and in one book. Jesus said "I am the way, the truth and the life." (John 14:6) There is only one way (via the cross), and one truth (Jesus as the eternal Word), and one life (Jesus the only source of life). However there is a proper way and an improper way to introduce children to truth. To approach children with the attitude that says in effect "I have carefully studied this out and have discovered absolute truth so listen carefully to what I say" is probably not the best approach. The better approach is to say in effect "Let's say that I might be wrong and that you might be wrong but this (the Bible) is right. Therefore, let's you and I study this book together so that we can come to the knowledge of the truth together." It is when children see that God has made an unlimited provision of soul salvation but a limited application of it that they see the need to make their decision to trust the word of God and Jesus Christ as Savior. This is the message of Romans 3:22 "Even the righteousness of God *which is* by faith of Jesus Christ unto all and upon all them that believe: for there is no difference:…" The righteousness of God that everyone needs to get to heaven is "unto all" (i.e. available to all) but it is only "upon all that believe." Soul salvation is available to everyone today by faith but it is only possessed by (upon) those that believe the gospel that "Christ died for our sins." Children grow to take ownership of their salvation when they have thoroughly checked it out for themselves and have found that the Word of God is true, that they can understand it, and that they can simply believe it and rest in it.

Children need to know their Enemy

There is a three fold enemy of the believer -- those being: the world, the flesh and the devil. Children need to know what was the origin of each, how they each operate, and to know how that threefold enemy can actually conspire together to deceive them. They need to see the world as the united desire of unsaved people to suppress the truth and to prevent God from enjoying His creation and His saints from having fellowship with Him. They need to see the flesh as something that actually dwells within them and seeks to simply gratify its own desires independent of God's interests. They also need to see the devil as a real person who has set his will against God and seeks to foil God's plan of redeeming man.

Children need a Community of Saints

The ideal for every Christian home is that it be a part of a larger Christian community – what we would call a local church. There is a cycle of godliness that comprises what Paul, the apostle of the Gentiles, calls "the mystery of godliness." He also calls it "the house of God, which is the church of the living God, the pillar and ground of the truth." This is what we call the local church as the work unit by which the church – the body of Christ works out of to evangelize the geographical area in which it exists.

> "But if I tarry long, that thou mayest know how thou oughtest to behave thyself in the house of God, which is the church of the living God, the pillar and ground of the truth. And without controversy great is the mystery of godliness: God was manifest in the flesh, justified in the Spirit, seen of angels, preached unto the Gentiles, believed on in the world, received up into glory." (I Timothy 3:15-16)

This local church when functioning properly becomes a family of families. The cycle of godliness goes like this: Sound doctrine produces strong saints. Strong saints produce strong families. Strong families support strong churches. Strong churches hold forth sound doctrine. Sound doctrine then produces strong saints and the cycle continues.

The importance of the local church is then evident as we recognize the importance of godly influences in the local church. However, there are some influences out there that we do not want in the local church community. Therefore, church discipline comes into play as a necessity for maintaining the purity of character in the local church. Thus the apostle of grace calls on the leaders of the local church (and the church at large) to maintain a certain minimum standard of performance as to conduct. The effectiveness of the local church in being the pillar and ground of the truth depends on not only its doctrinal integrity being in tact but also that it's moral and ethical standard of conduct be such as is needed to model godliness.

> "But now I have written unto you not to keep company, if any man that is called a brother be a fornicator, or covetous, or an idolater, or a railer, or a drunkard, or an extortioner; with such an one no not to eat." (1Corinthians 5:11)

What Children Need as they go into Adulthood:

There are some things that we need in life in growing into adulthood to be well rounded and fully functional as individuals. Let's consider some of these things:

- Children need a certain amount of autonomy – That being the ability to grow so as to act rather than to be acted upon. In Christ we, as believers, have the power to act through the working of the Holy Spirit. Though it be from a position of human weakness (2Cor. 12:9; Eph. 3:20; Phil. 2:13), we take actions based upon instructions in the Word of God.

- Children need knowledge – That being an accurate understanding of the real world (Col. 2:3; Phil. 3:7-9) as well as the knowledge of the working of God in the regenerated heart of believers. In the Pauline Epistles we have the knowledge that we need to function successfully as mature saints in the Dispensation of Grace (Eph. 3:1-9).

- Children wisdom -- need the ability to apply knowledge to real life situations. In Christ we have access to all of the treasures of wisdom and knowledge (Col. 2:3; Phil 3:7-9).

- Children need a sense of purpose. That would be an answer to the questions like: Who am I? Why am I here? What is my eternal destiny? In Christ we are a part of the eternal purpose that God has for man. Our children need to understand that God has a purpose for the human race of which they are part and that they can live out purposeful lives based on that understanding (Col. 3:11-12; Eph. 1:10; Heb. 2: 6 -7).

- Children need something to glory in. As believers we can glory in the Lord and in all that He is to us (1Cor. 1:31; Gal 6:14-15).

- Children need an active prayer life that gives them confidence that "things will be OK with me." In Christ, children learn that they have eternal security (Eph. 1:12 -13) and that they need not be overwhelmed by anxieties but they can take everything to God in prayer (Phil. 4:6-7). With an active prayer life and continual study of the Word, children learn that they can maintain a two way communication with God.

- Children need motivation that compels them to act and to live. The motivation that the grace of God gives people flows from knowing the love of Christ. Believers are constrained by the love of Christ and are motivated by His work of redemption on Calvary (2Cor. 5:7-17).

[17] Therefore if any man *be* in Christ, *he is* a new creature: old things are passed away; behold, all things are become new. [18] And all things *are* of God, who hath reconciled us to himself by Jesus Christ, and hath given to us the ministry of reconciliation; [19] To wit, that God was in Christ, reconciling the world unto himself, not imputing their trespasses unto them; and hath committed unto us the word of reconciliation. (2 Corinthians 5:17-19)

CHAPTER 2
OUR HUMAN MAKEUP AS CREATURES
CREATED IN THE IMAGE OF GOD

Man is created in the Image of God – "And God said, Let us make man in our image, after our likeness: and let them have dominion over the fish of the sea, and over the fowl of the air, and over the cattle, and over all the earth, and over every creeping thing that creepeth upon the earth. So God created man in his own image, in the image of God created he him; male and female created he them." (Genesis 1:26-27)

We understand from scripture that God is a trinity of three separate persons in the one Godhead. God is three in person but one in essence and being. In John 1:1 we find two separate persons both being referred to as God. In Acts 5:4 we find that the Holy Ghost is also called God. The Bible word for the trinity is the term "the Godhead." (Acts 17:29; Romans 1:20; Colossians 2:9) In Genesis 1:26 we find that God, in creating man, said "...Let us make man in in our image, after our likeness..." As we therefore study man, we would expect to find a trinitarian makeup of man as well. And we truly do so. The apostle's prayer for the Thessalonians states the case: "And the very God of peace sanctify you wholly; and I pray God your whole spirit and soul and body be preserved blameless unto the coming of our Lord Jesus Christ." (1Thessalonians 5:23) We mortal men are each a trinity of spirit, soul, and body. This trinitarian make up constitutes our likeness to God – though there is a difference in that we are each one person while God (the godhead) is one God but is three in person. Though the one godhead is three in person but one in number, He created one human race that is individually one in person but as a race is billions in number.

Though we each are singular (one in person), there are defined in the Bible three different mentalities in our makeup. The soul has a mentality that the Bible calls "the heart" (Romans 10:9 &10) where we make decisions in life (1Cor. 6:20). We are each a soul who has a body and who also has a spirit (1Cor. 6:20). The soul is the real person. It is the sum total of our affections and personality. It is the "youness" of you. It is what makes you "you." The mentality of our human spirit is what the Bible calls our mind. We actually make up our mind by what we (the soul) decide to put into it. As we put into our spirits the Word of God we form there in our spirit the mind of Christ (1Cor. 2:16). The spirit is given to us by God to enable us to relate to God and to be able (once it is regenerated and instructed by the Word of God) to think the way God thinks. Our physical body also has a mentality. The Bible calls the mentality of our physical body "the flesh." The flesh seeks to gratify its own desires. It is in our physical body in which we live in the physical world created by the eternal Word (John 1:1-4) that our sin nature resides (Romans 7:23).

The part of our makeup that is in the image of God is primarily in our soul. The apostle Paul tells us in 1Corinthians 6:20 "For ye are bought with a price: therefore glorify God in your body, and in your spirit, which are God's." Being a direct command, we understand that the subject is you – the soul that is you. This passage tells us that "you" are a soul who has a body and who also has a spirit and "you" (the soul that is you) decides what you will do with each. The apostle tells us in Romans 8:16 "The Spirit itself beareth witness with our spirit, that we are the children of God..." We understand from this passage that the Holy Spirit communicates with our human spirit via the written word of God. Our human spirit is given to us by God to enable us to receive the things of God and to understand divine concepts. This however, is only after the human spirit is regenerated by the Holy Spirit in response to the believer's personal faith in the redeeming shed blood of the Savior. It is in the soul that the Holy Spirit works to conform the believer to the image of Christ (Rom. 8:29).He does this as the believer gets into the Word of God to seek understanding and to yield to the revealed will of God as we find it in the Word of God

Believers conformed to the image of Christ

There are eight things that the Holy Spirit does in a person (at the very moment of conversion to Christ) when he or she trusts Jesus as Savior. We touched on them in the introduction. They are:

1) He circumcises that person with a spiritual circumcision (Col. 2:11-12);

2) He regenerates that person by putting life into that person's previously dormant spirit (Titus 3:5);

3) He indwells that person so as to maintain an instant access of that person to God (Rom. 8:11);

4) He baptizes the believer into Christ to join that person in a spiritual union to Christ to transfer the believer's sin to Christ and His righteousness to the believer and to form the Body of Christ;

5) He seals the believer to eternal life to insure eternal security (Eph. 1:13);

6) He washes the believer of the stain of sin;

7) He sanctifies to indicate ownership of the believer by God (1Cor. 6:19); and

8) He justifies the believer to impute righteousness to his spiritual account (2Cor. 5:21). These eight things are the initial work that the Holy Spirit does at the instant of soul salvation. At that point, He begins to work in the believer to conform him or her to the image of Christ. (Romans 8:28-29)

The work of grace in the believer

In the illustration below (Figure 2), there is a spiritual circumcision that actually separates the inward man of the soul and the spirit, both of which are redeemed at the moment of salvation, from the outward man (the physical body). Both the soul and spirit are redeemed at that instant of soul salvation but the body (the outward man) is not redeemed yet and will not be until the rapture (Rom. 8:23-24). The practical result of the spiritual circumcision is that what the sin nature does from that time on in the physical body will not be imputed to the charge of the believer (the soul of the believer) as far as his eternal destiny is concerned. The apostle quotes David regarding this imputed righteousness saying: "Blessed *are* they whose iniquities are forgiven, and whose sins are covered. [8] Blessed *is* the man to whom the Lord will not impute sin." Note the broader text of this passage:

> **Romans 4:4-8 (KJV)**
> "[4] Now to him that worketh is the reward not reckoned of grace, but of debt. [5] But to him that worketh not, but believeth on him that justifieth the ungodly, his faith is counted for righteousness. [6] Even as David also describeth the blessedness of the man, unto whom God imputeth righteousness without works, [7] *Saying,* Blessed *are* they whose iniquities are forgiven, and whose sins are covered. [8] Blessed *is* the man to whom the Lord will not impute sin."

The physical body is then the outward man that perishes (2Cor.4:16) but the soul and spirit constitute the inward man that is renewed day by day. In Chapter 3 we will look at how each of these three parts of our makeup is impacted by the growing up process. As parents, we need to be concerned about the entire person in each of our children.

Each part of our makeup (the spirit, the soul, and the body) gives the believer a certain consciousness. The spirit is the part of our makeup that gives us a consciousness of God and provides the means whereby God can communicate to us through His Word. There is a correspondence of our human spirit with the Spirit of God. We see this described in Romans 8:16-17 "The Spirit itself beareth witness with our spirit, that we are the children of God: [17] And if children, then heirs; heirs of God, and joint-heirs with Christ; if so be that we suffer with *him*, that we may be also glorified together." Our physical body gives us a world consciousness. We live in the physical world that was created by Christ and for Christ (Col. 2:10-12) by means of our physical body. Finally then, our soul is what gives us our personality – our self-consciousness or identity. It is who we are.

We do our thinking in our soul and our spirit. We make our decisions in our soul. We see this in 1Corinthians 6:19-20 where we are instructed the "glorify God in your body and in your spirit which are God's." The thought in that passage is that you are a soul who has a body and who has a spirit and the soul that is you decides what you will do with your body and your spirit both of which belong to God and to you as a new creature in Christ. We then carry out the decisions that we make in our soul through our physical body. The gray matter that we have in our heads (what we call our brain) is not where we do our thinking. Rather, it is what enables us to interface with and interact with the real world around us through our physical body and our five senses. Our brain is the seat of our talents in the physical skills such as music, art, craftsmanship, athletics, etc. It is interesting to note that the Bible says nothing about the amazing human brain. The brain, though it is a part of our physical makeup, is not an active part of our spiritual makeup.

Figure 1 below is an illustration of the relationship of God, man, and the physical universe. God exists out side of the space-matter-time continuum that we call the universe. God exists outside of it. Man was created to live in this physical creation. God has revealed Himself to us through book – the Bible. What man can know about God's eternal purposes and how we can relate to Him and interact with Him are found there. A further treatment of this concept is presented in the author's book *You and Your Creator*.

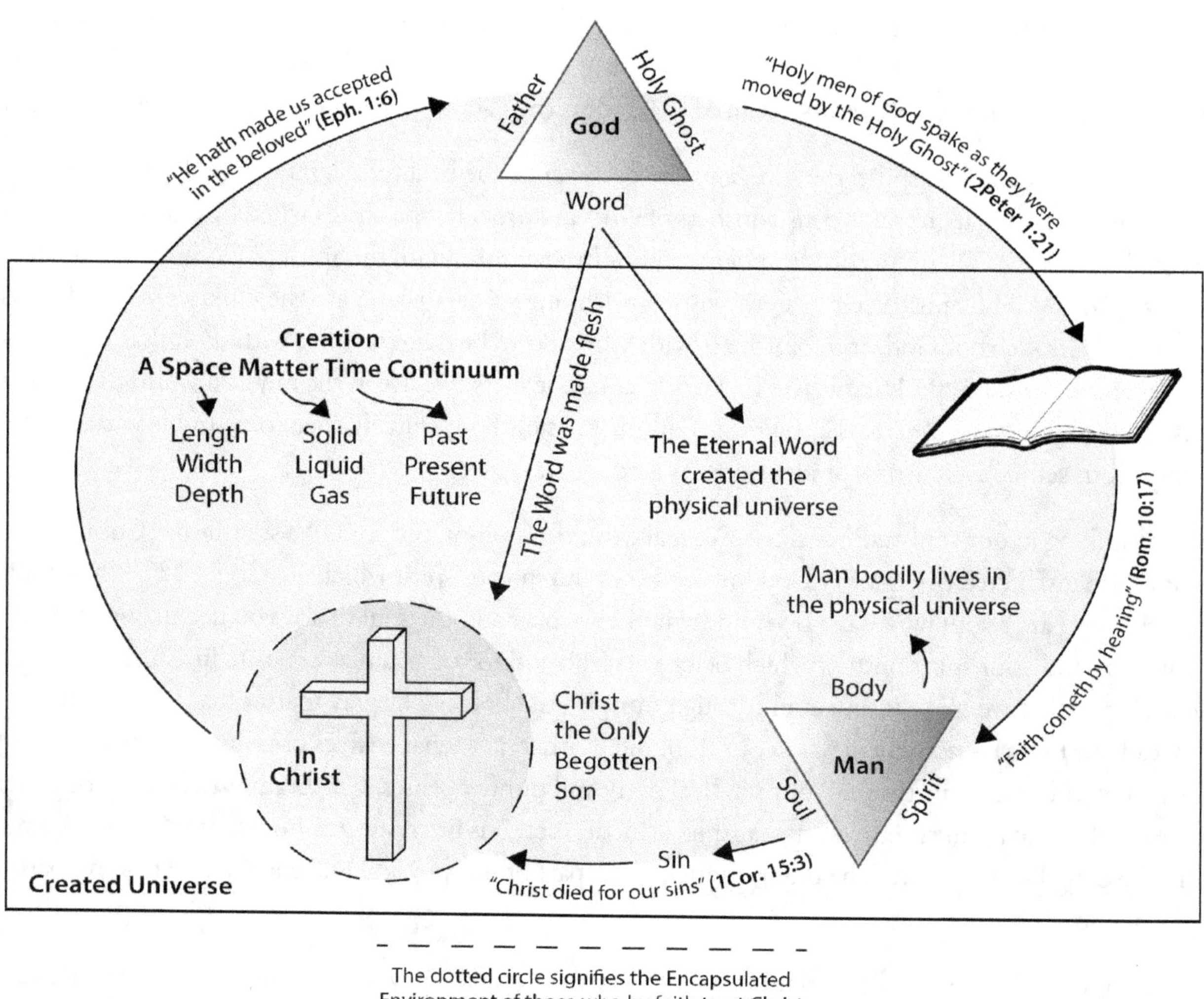

Figure 1 Man's Place in God's Created Universe

Figure 2 (below) illustrates the three part makeup of man, how each part is affected by conversion to Christ at regeneration, and the relationship of the inward man that is renewed day by day with the outward man that perishes. We encourage you the reader to check out the scripture references cited in their contexts to gain understanding in these important Bible concepts.

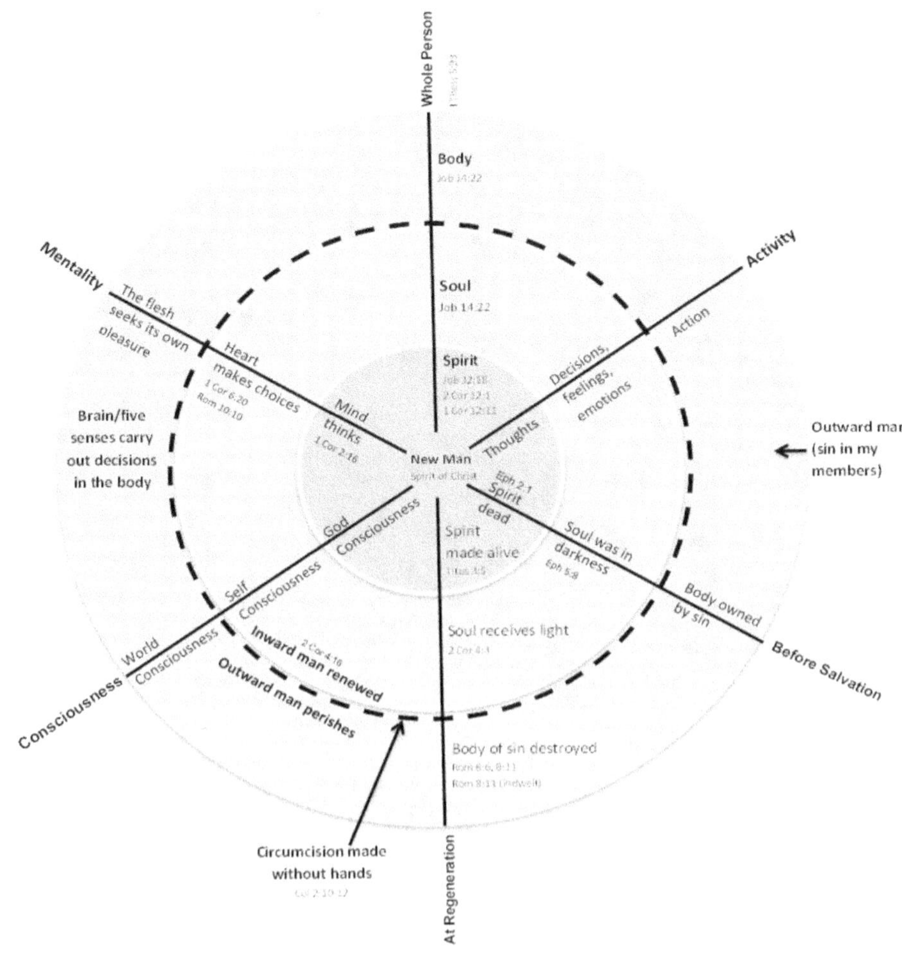

Figure 2 Our Three Part Human Makeup

Job 14:22 -- Job sees the soul as dwelling in the physical body. "But his flesh upon him shall have pain, and his soul within him shall mourn."

Job 32:18 sees the spirit of man dwelling within him – in the soul that is the man "For I am full of matter, the spirit within me constraineth me."

The soul and the spirit comprises what the Bible calls "the inwrd man" (2Cor. 4:16)

The Bible sees the physical body as the "Outward man that perishes." The apostle Paul says of the flesh "For I know that in me (that is, in my flesh,) dwelleth no good thing: for to will is present with me; but how to perform that which is good I find not." (Romans 7:18)

The Bible talks about a process of Regeneration that happens to a person when that individual makes a decision to trust in the redeeming work of the Lord Jesus Christ. That is the process that God the Holy Spirit performs at the instant one trusted Jesus Christ as Savior.

Titus 3:5-7 "5 Not by works of righteousness which we have done, but according to his mercy he saved us, by the washing of regeneration, and renewing of the Holy Ghost; 6 Which he shed on us abundantly through Jesus Christ our Saviour; 7 That being justified by his grace, we should be made heirs according to the hope of eternal life."

Regeneration affects the whole person (spirit, soul and body). Before salvation, the soul was in darkness (Eph. 5:8). At regeneration, the soul receives light (2Cor. 4:4). Before salvation, the spirit was dead and dormant (Eph. 2:1). At regeneration, the spirit is made alive and capable of receiving the things of the Spirit of God (1Cor. 2:15). Before salvation, the physical body was owned by the sin nature that dwells in it (Rom. 6:6). At regeneration, the physical body had a change of ownership. It now belongs to Christ who redeemed it (1Cor. 6:20), to the Holy Spirit who dwells in it (1Cor. 6:19) and to the believer who now lives the Christians life in it (Gal. 2:20). In the process of regeneration, the Holy Spirit performed a spiritual surgery called a "circumcision made without hands" (Col. 2:10-12) that separates the outward man that perishes from the inward man that is renewed day by day (2Cor. 4:16). At regeneration, the inward man (the soul and the spirit) was redeemed but the physical body will be redeemed at the rapture, the official adoption (Rom. 8:23).

CHAPTER 3
GRACE PARENTING: GROWTH AND DEVELOPMENT OF THE WHOLE PERSON

Leading the Child to Soul Salvation

The highest priority that we as believing parents have in the growth and development of our children is the presentation of the gospel to them that they might be converted to the Savior. It is apparent from passages as Romans 5:13; Matthew 18:3, 10, 14; 2Samuel 12:23; and Jonah 4:11-12 that children are in a "safe" state in infancy. (see the chapter in the author's book *You and Your Creator* on infant salvation) However, when they reach the age of accountability, they need to be "saved" from their sin's debt penalty in the sense of Ephesians 2:8-10. Because "...Faith cometh by hearing and hearing by the word of God..." (Romans 10:17), it is essential that the Bible be central in all spiritual dialogue with children. There are four attributes of God that children need to understand in order to make their decision to trust Jesus Christ as Savior. They are:

1. God is a loving God (John 3:16) who desires that all men be saved (1Cor. 1:18) and to come to the knowledge of the truth (1Tim. 2:4).

2. God is absolutely holy and therefore must be separate from sin. (Rom. 3:23)

3. God is a just God who must punish every sin (Romans 2:6-10). When all of the accounting for sin is done, there will be no sin left unpunished (2Cor. 5:21). The sin of the unbeliever is punished on the unbelieving soul in hell and the lake of fire (Rev. 21:8). The sin of the believer is punished in the redeeming work of Jesus Christ on the cross of Calvary (2Cor. 5:21)

4. God, being infinite in wisdom, came up with a plan whereby He can bring sinners into His presence without bringing sin with them. That plan involved God becoming a man, living a perfect human life, and then surrendering that life to pay sin's debt for every man. (Rom. 3: 23-26)

Children at that point need to understand that a decision on their part is needed for God to save them. They need to understand what it is that is to be believed (Romans 3:22).

The similitude of the farmer

Parenting has an interesting similitude to farming with regard to producing godly character. One key parallel between farming and instilling godly character is in the fact that you do not cram on a farm. Unless you sow when it is time to sow, you do not reap when it is time to reap. So it is with parenting from a Christian perspective when it comes to sowing and reaping. It is the basic Law of the Harvest:

> You reap what you sow;
> You reap more than you sow;
> You reap after you sow.

2Corinthians 9:6 "[6] *But this I say,* He which soweth sparingly shall reap also sparingly; and he which soweth bountifully shall reap also bountifully." (2Corinthians 9:6)

So it is with character. Character is the sum total of our habits. Character is sown through a life time of habits. Good habits form good character while bad habits become the form of bad character. Character can be changed but it involves the forming of different habits.

> Sow a thought and you reap an action;
> Sow actions and you reap a habit;
> Sow a habit and you reap a character;
> Sow a character and you reap a destiny [and a reputation].

A person's character is defined as all the things that a person does, what his affections are set on, and how he thinks. It is based on these that a person is judged by others as being of good character or bad. There are three factors in forming habits. They are: 1) knowing what to do; 2) gaining skill in doing it; and 3) having a desire to do it. Godly character (godliness) is actually God's character and personality being manifest in the lives of believers (1Tim. 3:16; Phil. 4:8). It is defined by the written Word of God working in the believer to conform the believer to God's Son (Romans 8:29). It consists of things as:

Honesty – Conforming our words to reality (Col. 3:9)

Integrity – Conforming reality to our words (Titus 2:7 – 10)

Temperance –Control of self (2Timothy 3:10-11)

    Control of the tongue (Titus 3:2; James 1:26; 3:5-6)

Courage (Romans 8:15; 2Tim. 1:7)

Justice (Titus 2:12)

Patience (1Thess. 5:15)

Dignity – Self respect as a child of God created in the image of God (Col. 3:12)

Purity (Titus 2:8; 2Cor. 7:1)

Goodness (Titus 3:8).

The similitude of the Archer

There is also a similitude of the archer to parenting. We see it in Psalm 127:3-5 "[3] Lo, children *are* an heritage of the LORD: *and* the fruit of the womb *is his* reward. [4] As arrows *are* in the hand of a mighty man; so *are* children of the youth. [5] Happy *is* the man that hath his quiver full of them: they shall not be ashamed, but they shall speak with the enemies in the gate." One fact that draws this similitude is that everything that a man will do in archery to insure that the arrow reaches its target he does before he releases the arrow. So it is with parenting. Everything that a man will do to instruct the children in godliness he does in those first 18 years of life and most of that is done in the formative years up to about age 6.

The Importance of Parental Example

God is interested in what we do. However, God is more interested in why we do what we do than He is in what we do.

The pattern for marriage is Christ and the Church (Eph. 5:25-33)

The pattern for parenthood is also Christ and the Church

- He confirms His love for us   (2 Cor. 5:17)

- He accepts us   (Eph 1:4-6)

- He builds us up   (Col 2:7)

- We are His workmanship   (Eph 2:10)

- He values us   (Eph 1:6,12,14)

- We are the fullness of Christ   (Eph 1:23;3:19)

- We are chastened of the Lord   (1Cor 11:32)

Let's talk about motives:

If we were to categorize the reasons for people to do the right thing (i.e. conducting oneself righteously or right in the eyes of others); all of those reasons would fall into one of three broad categories.

1. People can do the right thing (in the eyes of others) as a show for people to see. This would be in the realm of politics or religion. This is action taken not sincerely but to gain favor with others who are watching. This reasoning might produce the desired results but the motivation behind it is rooted in deceit.

2. People can do the right thing to satisfy an emotional need. This might be action taken to satisfy a man's personal integrity or to maintain a good name for the sake of feeling good about oneself. Here again the results are correct but the reasoning though honest is nonetheless self-serving.

3. People can do the right thing to bring honor and glory to God. This would be grace in action. This is the motivation of 2Corinthians 5:14 and 15 "For the love of Christ constraineth us because we thus judge, that if one died for all, then all were dead: And that he died for all that they should not henceforth live unto themselves but unto him which died for them and rose again." Here we come to the highest form of positive motivation – to bring honor to the Savior out of a thankful heart for His redeeming work.

As we speak of parental example, we need to consider this breakdown of the motivation by which we act in our lives. We made the point earlier that godliness is as much caught as it is taught. Our children will model our attitudes as surely as they will model our actions. In the chart below, I attempt to illustrate these three motivations for doing right.

The bottom axis would be time. The left (vertical) axis is the proportion of the motivation within the heart of a child

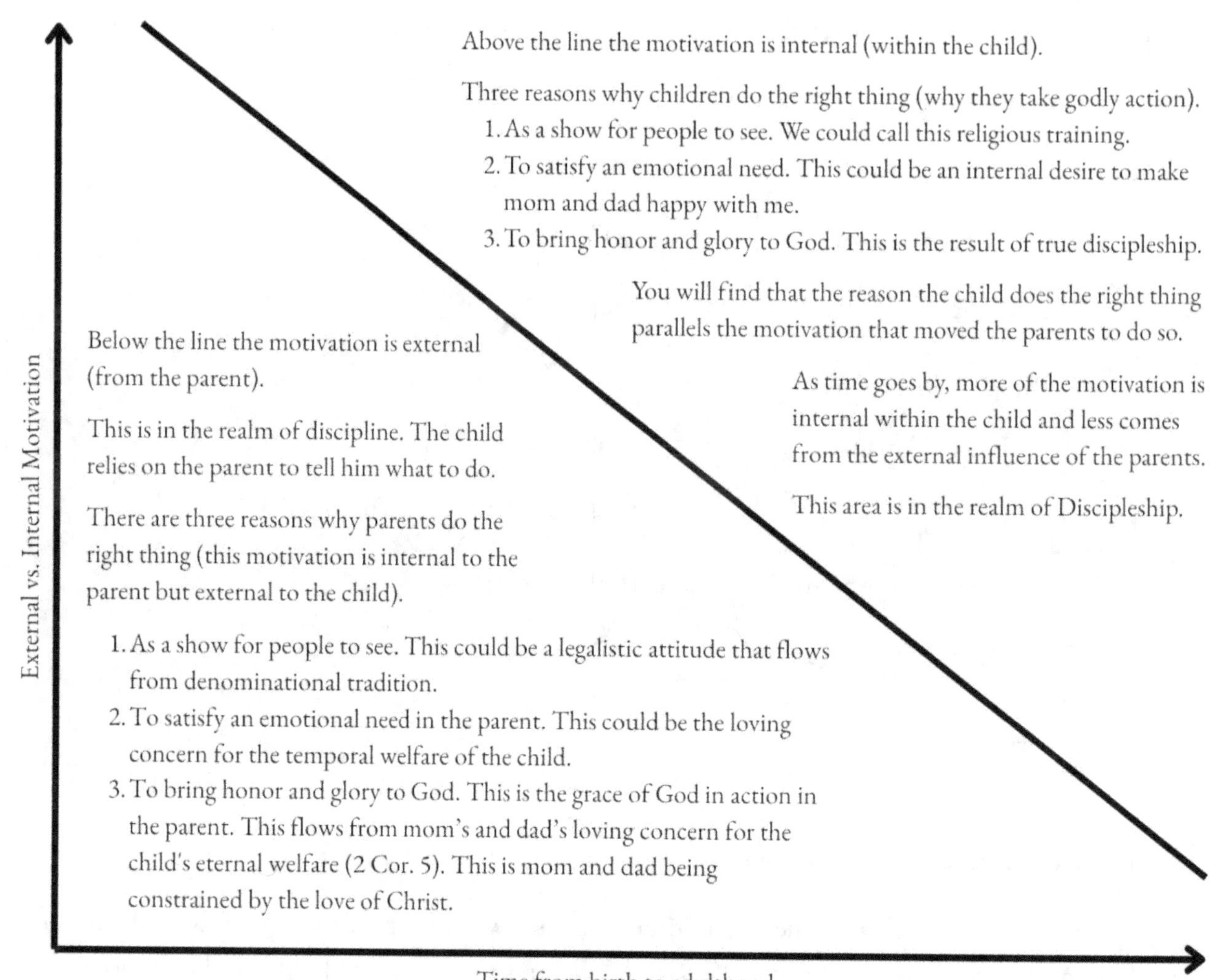

Figure 3:
Time increases from left to right to represent growth of children and the effect of parental influence on motivation. Below the sloped line we see the external influence of parents on a child's motivation to do right. Above the line, we see the child's internal (intrinsic) motivation. The vertical axis is the degree of motivation. It can be internal as being within the child or external as coming from the parents.

to conduct himself righteously as he grows to adulthood that comes from the external influence of the parents and the proportion that is attributed to the internal motivation within the child. Doubtless there is a certain amount of motivation of all parents in each of these three categories. Doubtless also, the same proportion of each these three reasons to act righteously will show up in the child as time goes on. Such is the strong influence of parents. The ideal though is that the motivation of the son or daughter be rooted in true spiritual maturity of a heart desire to bring honor to God. Why we do what we do in more important to character development that what we actually do. How much more likely that is to happen if that same motivation is resident in mom and dad!

As we talk about the ideal, let's consider the growing up process from a realistic perspective. As we start out with a child at birth and mark the stages of development, we realize that it is truly a work in progress. In the table below we picture what we might view as the process. As we said at the outset of our study, this process will require an all hands on deck effort of "submitting yourselves one to another in the fear of God. Wives submit yourselves unto your own husbands as unto the Lord... Husbands love your wives even as Christ also loved the church and gave himself for it... Children obey your parents in the Lord...And ye fathers provoke not your children to wrath: but; but bring them up in the nurture and admonition of the Lord." (Eph. 5:21 to 6:4).

Table 1 Growing from Birth to Spirit Filled Adulthood

At Birth	In Adolescence	Spirit Filled, Christ Centered Adulthood
Selfish Self Centered Totally Absorbed with Self	Others Centered Maturing in Decision Making Able to face teen years successfully Learning to deal with: Insecurity Developing Sex drive Unstable Emotions Rebellion Seeking Approval Finding themselves	God Centered Christ Centered Has the mind of Christ being instructed from the Word rightly divided. Knows how to avoid the walk after the flesh and how to be filled with the Spirit. The focus is on the eternal values of the life of Christ.

Godly Growth and Development: God has assigned to each of us a life span of about 80 years +/-. During that time, we grow from total dependence through independence to interdependence.

Interdependence

Independence

Dependence

Dependence – This is how every child enters our home – how we all start out in life.

Physically: *I need you to provide for my physical needs.*

Emotionally: *My sense of worth comes from your opinion of me.*

Spiritually: *I depend on you to tell me what to think*

Independence – Empowers us to act rather than be acted upon.

Physically: *I can take care of myself and I take responsibility to do so.*

Emotionally: *I have intrinsic worth as a person for whom Christ died and redeemed.*

Spiritually: *I get my guidance from the Word of God. I have searched it out for myself and found it to be absolute truth. I grow in wisdom as I apply godly principles to my life.*

Interdependence - Equips us for the reality of family, fellowship, leadership, etc.

Physically: *I am independent but I know that two of us can do more than twice as much as each of us working alone.*

Emotionally: *I have my own sense of worth but I also have a need to love, to give, and to receive love from others.*

Spiritually: *I can think for myself but I also know that I, together with my brothers and sisters in Christ, can work together to encourage each other, to be encouraged by each other, and to reach out to others with the soul saving Word of God.*

Grace Living – An Affair of the Heart

Grace Parenting is therefore the wholesome development of the whole person. Figure 2 (in Chapter 2) illustrates the information presented below.

1. There is more to man than what meets the eye. Each of the three parts of our makeup has a mentality that can be identified in the Bible.

    a. There is a Spirit within man (Job 32:8) / The mentality of our spirit is what the Bible calls our Mind (Rom. 8:27)

    b. The Soul is the real person (Job 14:22) / The mentality of the soul is what the Bible calls the Heart (1Sam. 16:7; Prov. 21:7).

    c. The Body is the temporary residence of the soul (Rom. 6:6; 2Cor. 5:1) / The Bible calls the mentality of our body the Flesh (Gal. 5:16)

2. The Lord looks on the heart (1Sam. 16:7) but what is the "Heart"?

    a. Our emotions reside there in the heart:

        i. Sorrow (Psalm 13:2)

        ii. Joy (Psalm 13:5)

        iii. Fear (Psalm 27:2).

    b. We speak to ourselves there (Psalm 14:1; 53:1).

    c. Humility resides there as does pride (Psalm 34:18 cf 51:17).

    d. We establish our purposes in life there (2Cor. 9:7).

    e. We keep our secrets there (1Cor. 14:23).

    f. We believe with the heart (Rom. 10:6-16).

    g. We obey with the heart (Rom. 6:17).

    h. We Serve with the heart (Eph. 6:5&6).

We can now give a definition: "The heart of a man is the sum total of the affections that he has developed and established within his soul based upon the decisions that he (his soul) had made."

3. The heart of the Natural man:

    a. Is Darkened (Rom. 1:21)

    b. Is Impenitent (Rom. 2:5)

    c. Is Blinded (Eph. 4:18).

4. At Conversion the Word works on the heart (Heb. 4:12).

    a. The heart is that part of our makeup that believes (Rom. 10: 9&10).

    b. The veil of unbelief is removed from the heart (2Cor. 3:15-18).

5. You (your soul – the entity that is you) decides what you believe (1Cor. 6:19) and then what you believe produces your heart's affections (Prov. 23:7).

6. The joy of the Lord then fills the heart that is tuned to the Lord (Eph. 6:19).

Forgiveness and the work of the Spirit in the heart

What is forgiveness? True forgiveness is an act of the will – not an act of the emotions. Forgiveness is done in faith before God and is motivated by a love for the offending party that comes from God. A person forgives in a conscious decision to release an offending party from any debt that he perceives to be owed to him by an offence (whether that offence is real or imagined). Forgiveness is accompanied with a resolve that the matter is cleared and you have chosen that the matter will never be an issue with that party again. That is not to say that we will automatically trust the offending party – especially if the offence is likely to happen again. Forgiveness is a decision made in our soul and is a matter of a heart decision. Trust however is a matter of our spirit – where we store the knowledge by which we make decisions. Our emotions are the first responders in us that get our attention. However, we must not act out of our emotions. We must think above our emotions if we are to make sound decisions. Our emotions (the right emotions if we act correctly according to the Word of God) will then follow our actions.

Who can truly forgive? The only person who can truly forgive is a person who has experienced true forgiveness himself. For the believer, this is a faith application of 2Corinthians 5:14-15 "[14] For the love of Christ constraineth us; because we thus judge, that if one died for all, then were all dead: [15] And *that* he died for all, that they which live should not henceforth live unto themselves, but unto him which died for them, and rose again."

What is the Biblical pattern for forgiveness? The Bible pattern for forgiveness is God's forgiveness to us (Eph. 4:32). "God commendeth His love for us in the while we were yet sinners, Christ died for us" (Rom. 5:6).

Is forgiveness dependent upon the offending party seeking forgiveness? No! Not in the Dispensation of Grace (See Ephesians 4:32 – 5:2 below). In the kingdom program (i.e. in God's program with Israel) there was a difference (Luke 17: 3-4). There is a difference between forgiveness and trust. Trust can be restored when the offending party seeks forgiveness. Without repentance, the offence will likely happen again. In a family unit, the lines of communication must stay open. There needs to be the communication of love for the offending party with the evidence that the offence is forgiven. However, the forgiveness is not to eliminate the need for corrective action if the offence is disobedience on the part of a child.

There is a correct and a wrong paradigm in the act of forgiveness. To think about a wrong that has been done to us and asking ourselves "how do I feel about this?" and then acting on my feelings is the wrong paradigm. However, asking ourselves "What does the Word of God have to say about how I should respond to this?" is the correct thinking that will lead to true forgiveness. Forgiveness done out of our thinking based on the Word of God will lead to positive emotions following our thinking. Here again healthy emotions follow proper actions taken based on the Word of God. A forgiving person is an emotionally stable, mature person.

Ephesians 4:31-32

[31] Let all bitterness, and wrath, and anger, and clamour, and evil speaking, be put away from you, with all malice: [32] And be ye kind one to another, tenderhearted, forgiving one another, even as God for Christ›s sake hath forgiven you.

Ephesians 5:1-2 goes on to say: "[1] Be ye therefore followers of God, as dear children; [2] And walk in love, as Christ also hath loved us, and hath given himself for us an offering and a sacrifice to God for a sweetsmelling savour."

Note that forgiveness produces the healthy characteristics of kindness and tenderheartedness. On the other hand, a failure to forgive produces the negative emotions of bitterness, wrath and anger. An unforgiving spirit will make us a slave to the person we perceive to have wronged us. There is a sense in which that person owns us. You allow that person to live in your mind and occupy your thoughts.

There are some actions that are passed off as forgiveness but are not true forgiveness. Such actions do not give you the release that true forgiveness gives. I list some of those actions here from a CD set *Forgiveness Matters* by Richard Jordan of the Grace School of the Bible:

- To simply excuse the action is not true forgiveness. To do so is to refuse to reprove sin for what it is (Eph. 5:10-17).

- To deny the action is not forgiveness. To do so is a lie to both the offending party and to the offended party. This eventually leads to a twisted sense of reality and to a distorted sense of what is hurtful and what is not.

- To merely accept the actions or the wrong is not forgiveness. To do so would be to say to your self that you deserve such treatment. This leads to a dangerous belittling of self.

- To tolerate the action or the wrong or to resolve to simply endure it is not forgiveness. To do so would be to tolerate being abused or mistreated. Healthy interpersonal relationships have boundaries that are mutually recognized and respected.

- To explain the action away is not forgiveness. To do so would be to inhibit the work of the Holy Spirit to work in your life and the life of the other person to effect a positive change.

A pure heart is a heart that is so filled with the things of the Lord that there is no room for the things of the flesh. There are three main factors that form our person – who we are. These influences are summarized in the Table 2 below.

Table 2: The Nurture and Admonition of the Lord in Ephesians 6:4

Nature is what comes naturally by birth	**Nurture basically comes from mom and dad – our home and our culture**	**Scripture -- Maturity based on what we internalize into our soul and spirit from the Word of God**
Nature provides this. We have no choice in the matter. We are born with a given temperament and also with a sin nature.	Our parents, our environment, and our culture provide this nurturing. We have very little to do with this but to endure it and live with it.	Individual responsibility really starts here. Here is where the grace of God can work in our lives. Here is where positive change happens.
	But! As believing parents we have the power to look at the parenting that we had in light of the Scripture and give our children the benefit of grace living through the parenting that we provide to them.	Here is where an understanding of the Word rightly divided and the true spirituality that can and will correct any shortcomings in Nature and what Nurturing we had. This spiritual maturing comes from the faith application of the Word by which believers are enabled to "...judge all things..." (1Cor 2:13-16) and make decisions in life having "...the mind of Christ." Coming to spiritual maturity can not happen until we step back and take a close look at our lives and ask the penetrating question: "What areas of my life are not conformed to Christ (i.e. not conformed to the will of God as revealed in the Word of God)?"

Note: It is a basic fact of life that hurting people (people who are hurting) tend to hurt other people. Sin (our old man – the sin nature) will consider any hurt (whether real or imagined) and will internalize it and respond destructively. It will produce anger, bitterness, resentment, adultery, drunkenness and other works of the flesh (Gal. 5:19-

21) in our hearts. If not dealt with it will produce any number of what might be called neurosis in us. But there is a healing available for the hurt soul in the grace of God. That healing of our souls (i.e. our person) can be ours by a faith acceptance and application of the doctrines of grace. The doctrine starts with the understanding that we as believers have been totally forgiven by God in Christ (Romans Chapters 1 thru 5) and are secure in Him. It then teaches us that we can, in like manner, so also forgive others (Ephesians 4:31 & 32). That healing also includes the knowledge of the fact our sin nature is no longer our master (Romans 6 thru 8) but rather we are true sons of God in whom the Spirit of God is working to conform us to the image of His Son. We will study how grace works in the inner man in Chapter 4.

The Formula for Parenting (Nurturing = Diet + Discipline + Discipleship)

There are three components to the nurturing process: Diet (what is fed); Discipline (instilling strength of character), and Discipleship (conforming one's life to the image of God's Son by the application of grace doctrine).

Table 3

Diet	Discipline	Discipleship

To Feed the Whole Person:
1. Physical needs
  a. Food
  b. Clothing
  c. Shelter
2. Emotional Needs
  a. To Be Loved
  b. To be Valued
  c. To be recognized as a unique person in God's Kingdom (not a special person)
3. Spiritual Needs
 	
To provide spiritual leadership and direction to lead a child to the person and work of Christ. It is then up to the child to make the decisions.
	To develop the child's character and personality with regard to the indwelling sin nature.
	
	This involves both positive and negative reinforcement:
	
	Positive:
	
	• Parental Example
	• Instruction
	• Approval of things that are excellent
	• Celebration of success.
	
	Negative:
	
	• Chastening
	• Punishment
	• Discipline
	
	Not all discipline is equal. There is good discipline and bad discipline.
		To equip your child to live eternal life now while in this life.
		
		Discipleship involves three things:
		
		1. Study of the Word rightly divided.
		2. A vital, consistent, and continuous prayer life.
		3. Active fellowship with fellow believers (who also understand the Word rightly divided).
		
		Ideally this is the life of Christ in the parent reproduced in the lives of the children. In a real sense, spirituality is as much caught as it is taught.
		
		We have made mention several times of the "Word Rightly Divided" in our study. Appendix 5 addresses that concept.

The Nurture and Admonition of the Lord

Ephesians 6:4 "⁴ And, ye fathers, provoke not your children to wrath: but bring them up in the nurture and admonition of the Lord." But this passage (Eph. 6:4 cf. Col 3:21) contains a note of warning. It warns of the wrong kind of discipline.

We stop to ask an important question at this point. Who owns the kids? I have heard lots of claims of ownership of the kids from various sources. In some countries the state claims ownership. Even in America in recent years we hear of parents being regarded as terrorists for speaking out against things that are propaganda to change children's views on themselves and their country. That includes things like gender confusion and this critical race theory we hear about. To set the record straight, kids do not belong to the state, not to the school board, and not to any governmental agency or society at large or to any church. I quote Ezekiel 18:4 "⁴ Behold, all souls are mine; as the soul of the father, so also the soul of the son is mine: the soul that sinneth, it shall die." This makes it clear that all souls belong to the creator. We are created in His image. Just as surely as the coin that held Caesar's image belonged to Caesar (Matt. 22:21), so man which holds God's image (Gen. 1:26) belongs to God. Paul tells us in 1Corinthians 6:19-20 "¹⁹ What? know ye not that your body is the temple of the Holy Ghost *which is* in you, which ye have of God, and ye are not your own? ²⁰ For ye are bought with a price: therefore glorify God in your body, and in your spirit, which are God›s." Based on this, we understand that kids don't even technically belong to the parents but rather to God. However, as parents, we are charged by God with the responsibility to bring the kids up in the nurture and admonition of the Lord. That means that we as parents do have God given authority over them to guide their growth and development.

The Oppositions of Science Falsely So Called

Paul closes his epistle to the young man Timothy (and to us) with the words: "O Timothy, keep that which is committed to thy trust, avoiding profane *and* vain babblings, and oppositions of science falsely so called: Which some professing have erred concerning the faith. Grace *be* with thee. Amen." (1Timothy 6:20-21) Obviously Paul was greatly concerned about the influence false science would have on this young man. The great danger of a false science is that it is presented as truth and can be accepted as truth without being challenged or questioned. We see that as a very real existential threat to the spiritual welfare of people both young and old today. We today can put journalism in the same basket of deceitful practices employed by deceivers who professionally prepare documentation to trick people into believing lies and accepting false concepts in the guise of scholarly researched work. It takes someone skilled in critical thinking to discern and differentiate truth from error when error is packaged in what we assume to be actual validated information. For example, colleges and essentially all of academia and much of social media (You Tube being a case in point) presents organic evolution as a truth not to be questioned in spite of the fact that evolution has never been observed anywhere on earth at any time nor has organic evolution ever been proven.

If kids are going to develop a Christian world view, they will have to get it from an objective search for truth from a Bible-based curriculum that is taught by parents who are totally absorbed by Christ-like thinking. The following seven points has been gleaned from the web page foundationworldview.com." The web page and the curriculum were developed by Elizabeth Urbanowicz. She had been a teacher for 10 years teaching elementary students at a Christian school. She observed that despite being raised in a Christian home, attending a Christian school, and being active in church, her students thought more like the culture than like Christ. Her thoughts here are worthy of our consideration as parents:

Lies Children Believe

1. Children are conditioned by modern day education that truth is subjective. They therefore adopt the attitude that "If I believe it, it must be true."

    a. The problem with that line of thinking is that they do not develop critical thinking skills.

    b. Another problem is that kids fail to understand that there is such a thing as absolute truth.

2. Children are told that they "...should follow their heart."

    a. The problem is that "....the heart is ...deceitful above all things, and desperately wicked: who can know it?" (Jeremiah 17:9). Therefore, in this line of thinking, decisions are made based on emotions and not made out of the spiritual thinking process.

    b. Children need to understand that emotions are not the driver of critical thinking but rather they are designed by God to follow logical thinking.

3. Children are immersed into a worldly attitude that "Love affirms everything that I feel." The problem is that feelings are subjective but truth is objective (unchanging). Love compels us to be honest with one another and call error for what it is.

4. Children are conditioned by the world to think that faith is the opposite of knowledge. They are therefore conditioned to adopt the paradigm:

    a. "I go to school and I turn my mind on."

    b. "I go to church and I turn my mind off."

5. Children are told by secular sources that "Humans are a product of blind unguided evolution." They hold that view because the public education system, the entertainment industry, main stream media, academia, and public institutions teach and hold without question the theory of evolution without thought to a creator. This in spite of the fact there is no empirical evidence which has ever verified that one species ever evolved into another.

6. Children are told "You are what you have been waiting for. You are enough; you determine your own destiny; you rescue yourself; you have all that you need within yourself." The problem is that real truth comes from God but in our flesh dwells no good thing (Romans 7:18).

7. Children are told "A good God would not judge." Kids are constantly being told "Don't Judge." Yet believers are instructed to have discernment with regard to what is acceptable conduct for believers (1Cor. 5:11).

Parents need to understand that it is not about teaching children what to think but rather about teaching them how to think critically. They need to learn how to ask good questions.

The Family and Entertainment:

One of the areas of family life that needs to be shared is the view that the family takes towards Hollywood and the entire entertainment industry. One of the best ways to get to the same page with movies is for the family of mom, dad, and the kids to watch movies together and do an evaluation of the movie just watched. This takes some agreement ahead of time so that all are on board with what is to be done. Such an exercise in critical thinking is a valuable skill that children will learn to appreciate and will take it with them through life. It will also teach them how deceptive and seductive the world can be. The questionnaire below provides an excellent format for family evaluation of movies.

Family Evaluation of Movies

The threefold enemies of the believer are: the world, the flesh, and the devil. This three fold enemy attacks the family through the entertainment that we take in. One of the best ways to teach critical thinking skills to children is to evaluate movies together. The following can be a check list by which a movie is rated as to wholesomeness.

1. Does the movie make sin look attractive? How?

2. Does it promote a wholesome lifestyle? How or how not?

3. Does the program make fun of or ridicule the Lord Jesus Christ or the Word of God?

4. Does it emphasize fantasy?

5. What kind of character is exemplified by the main actors? Is this a good role model?

6. How does it square with Philippians 4:8?

7. Can I have meaningful devotion immediately after watching this movie?

8. As a believer, does this program appeal to my old man (my sin nature) or to the new man?

9. How did the movie affect me? What was my frame of mind after watching it?

10. How is the world portrayed? Is it portrayed as a dangerous place or as a place not to be feared?

11. Does the movie leave me thinking that man can do anything he sets his mind to?

12. How are problems solved in the movie?
By hurting others? -- By cooperation? -- By revenge? -- With Faith? -- With money? -- With communication? -- With magic? -- By worldly principles? -- By Biblical principles?

Family Evaluation of Music

We will be considering music in some detail in Chapter 10. However, for reference as music relates to entertainment, I list here ten prevalent themes of what we call rock music:

1. Rebellion

2. Violence

3. Nihilism

4. Escapism

5. Sex

6. Drugs

7. Suicide

8. Witchcraft

9. Satanic affirmation

10. Anti God and antichrist blasphemies

There are also four prevalent themes of country music that are equally negative influences on character:

1. Divorce

2. Drinking and Drunkenness

3. Adultery

CHAPTER 4
GRACE AND THE INNER MAN
(ROMANS CHAPTERS 6, 7 AND 8)

Grace in the Inner man and the Law

> **Romans 8:1-4 (KJV)** [1] *There is* therefore now no condemnation to them which are in Christ Jesus, who walk not after the flesh, but after the Spirit. [2] For the law of the Spirit of life in Christ Jesus hath made me free from the law of sin and death. [3] For what the law could not do, in that it was weak through the flesh, God sending his own Son in the likeness of sinful flesh, and for sin, condemned sin in the flesh: [4] That the righteousness of the law might be fulfilled in us, who walk not after the flesh, but after the Spirit.

The subject of Verse 1 of this passage is condemnation. In order to understand this passage of scripture; we need to identify what condemnation this is referring to. Chapter 8 of Romans is a summary of the two chapters before it. The immediate context identifies it as the condemnation that we saw in Chapter 7. To understand these four verses, we need to understand the terms. First we note that there are three different laws referenced. Let's list them and define them:

1. "The Law of the Spirit of life in Christ Jesus…" in Verse 2 is the principle of the Holy Spirit of God working in the regenerated spirit of the believer to produce the life of Christ in the believer. This is Galatians 2:20 in action.

2. "The Law of sin and death…" (Also referenced in Verse 2) is the principle of the indwelling sin nature that seeks to work through the flesh to produce spiritual death in the individual.

3. The third law (in Verses 3 and 4) is the Law of Moses which demanded righteous conduct from those who were under it but which it could not produce it because of the weakness of human flesh.

What does it mean to walk After the Spirit?

Perhaps the most critical point of doctrine that husbands and wives need to get a hold of is the doctrine of grace as a divine operating principle for the Dispensation of Grace in which we live. In Romans 8:2 Paul says that "…the law of the spirit of life in Christ Jesus has made me free from the law of sin and death." Grace works in the inner man of the heart (Romans 6 & 7). Where sin (referring to both that which we call the sin nature and sin, the action) abounded, grace did much more abound (Romans 5:20). Ultimately, it is only the grace of God that can defeat sin in the human race. Therefore, it is critically important that parents understand how grace works, apply it to their lives, and then to teach that doctrine of grace to their children. In the teaching of that doctrine, we are talking about first putting grace on display in our lives as parents and then to explain it in didactic terms to our children as they grow and mature to receive instruction.

The Walk after the Spirit – an Expose of Romans Chapter 6

The first fourteen verses of Chapter 6 of Romans lay out for believers how grace works in them to enable believers to live lives separated from sin unto God. These verses comprise the simple and basic doctrine that enables the believer to live a life free from the dominion and tyranny of the sin nature. That freedom comes by faith in the operation of God in baptizing believers into Christ's death, burial, and resurrection. The Holy Spirit performs that baptism in believers at the moment lost sinners trust Christ. He (the Holy Spirit) joins believers to Jesus Christ and indeed places them into an eternal, living relationship with Him. In that baptism, believers are so joined to Christ that they are members of His body, His flesh, and His bones much like how a man and a woman are joined in marriage (Ephesians 5:30).

The point to note, though, is that when He receives us as members of His body, He receives our sin so that it (our sin) actually becomes His, in that what was ours becomes His. He then, having acquired our sin and guilt by virtue of this baptism, could then apply the merits of His death, burial, and resurrection to pay the debt of our sin and to give us new life. He is the only one that could do that because He is the only one who did not have sin of His own that needed to be atoned for. This He did on the cross of Calvary. This baptism is referenced in Colossians 2:12, where we see that this baptism is "the operation of God." In 1Corinthians 12:13, we see that the Holy Spirit performs this baptism. But here in Romans 6 we see that this baptism has results that go beyond simply transferring our sin and guilt to the Savior so He could pay its debt. As a result of this baptism, our old man (i.e. our souls under the rule of our sin nature) has been crucified with Christ so we can now lead a different life than we did before. The end result is that we "are dead to sin" (Verse 2). Paul therefore asks (and answers) the rhetorical question of Verse 1.

Shall We Continue in Sin That Grace May Abound?

The following is an expository study of Romans Chapter 6. Follow the annotation note [a] to the annotations below for an in depth study of the passage.

> [1] What shall we say then? Shall we continue[a] in sin[b], that grace may abound? [2] God forbid. How shall we, that are dead to sin, live any longer therein? [3] Know ye not, that so many of us as were baptized[c] into Jesus Christ were baptized into his death? [4] Therefore we are buried[d] with him by baptism into death: that like as Christ was raised[e] up from the dead by the glory of the Father, even so we also should walk in newness of life. (Romans 6:1–4)

[a] The question raised in Verse 1 ("Shall we continue in sin, that grace may abound?") addresses a common objection thrown out against the gospel by those who seek to verbalize their objection to grace. If salvation is by grace through faith apart from works, then people could do anything they want and still be saved. Because soul salvation (i.e., having eternal life) is a gift of God (which Verse 23 says it is), then truly people who have accepted that gift can do whatever they want and still be saved (in the sense of being saved from sin's debt penalty in the lake of fire). However, the truth is that grace doesn't save people *to* sin but rather it saves them *from* sin. Apparently people were accusing Paul of making the argument that where sin abounded, grace super-abounded; then the more one sinned, the more grace there was (according to this argument), and the more God was glorified. Paul's answer to that false accusation that we should continue in sin that grace may abound was an emphatic statement: "God forbid." Nothing could be further from the truth.

[b] In this chapter, Paul often uses the figure of speech of personification. Personification is the imparting of personality to an inanimate thing for discussion purposes. The names given to the two natures in this passage are very informative. Here in Verse 1 "sin" is the old sin nature. Mr. Sin used to run our lives and used to (before we were justified by faith) actually owned our physical bodies. We will see more on this issue later.

Names for the old man:

- "Sin" (Verses 1, 2, 6–7, 10–12, 14, 16–18, 20, 23)

- "Our old man" (Verse 6)

- "Uncleanness" (Verse 19)

- "Iniquity" (Verse 19)

- "Death" (Verse 9)

Names for the new man:

- "Obedience" (Verse 16)

Names for the inner man (Ephesians 3:16):

- "Righteousness" (Verses 18–20)

- "The inward man" (2 Corinthians 4:16)

[c] The believer was baptized into Jesus Christ by the Holy Spirit at the very instant he or she trusted in Jesus Christ as Savior (1 Corinthians 12:3; Colossians 2:12). This baptism has nothing to do with water or speaking in tongues. This baptism isn't Pentecostal baptism, where Christ baptized the believers of Israel *with* "the Holy Spirit" (Matthew 3:4). This baptism is done *by* the Holy Spirit whereby sinners today in the dispensation of grace are baptized *into* Christ when we trusted Him as Savior. This baptism of Romans 6:3 is done by the Holy Spirit in response to our faith. "For ye are all the children of God by faith in Christ Jesus. For as many of you as have been baptized into Christ have put on Christ" (Galatians 3:26–27). The common misconception among professing believers today is

that baptism refers to either a water rite or to speaking in tongues, but there are many other baptisms in the New Testament. The organic meaning of baptism in the sense used here is to be identified with someone or something.

- Our Lord's death is referred to as a baptism (Matthew 20:22–23). Jesus Christ died a death that He did not have to die. Physical death is the result of sin and He had no sin of His own. He did die though because He took our sin upon Himself.

- There was a baptism unto Moses (1 Corinthians 10:2). Israel as a nation came out of Egypt following Moses but they could have turned back – until they crossed the Red Sea. Once they crossed the Red Sea, there was no turning back option anymore. The people and their leader were one. They were totally identified with Moses hence the term "baptized onto Moses."

- John the Baptist talked about a baptism with fire (Matthew 3:11). This is a baptism that would purge the unbelievers of Israel out from the nation. This is a matter of the unbelievers being identified with fire of judgment as the chaff is gathered and burned (Matthew 3:12) while the wheat represents the believers of Israel gathered into the kingdom.

- The baptism that John the Baptist practiced in was a water rite based on Numbers 19 and was "the baptism of repentance for the remission of sins" (Mark 1:4; Luke 3:3).

This baptism of Romans 6:1-4 is a baptism *into* Christ. Note that it's *not* a baptism into *water*, not a baptism *by* water, nor a baptism *with* the Holy Spirit, as was the case in Matthew 3:11. It's a baptism that the Holy Spirit performs. In Israel's program, there was a water rite required for salvation. "He that believeth *and is baptized* shall be saved; but he that believeth not shall be damned" (Mark 16:16, emphasis added). Nowhere in Paul's epistles, however, do we find a reference to water baptism as a requirement for salvation. In quite the opposite terms, Paul says. "Christ sent me not to baptize but to preach the gospel" (1 Corinthians 1:17). The only baptism Paul preached was the baptism the Holy Spirit performed in the process of forming the church, which is Christ's body (1 Corinthians 12:13, 27; Ephesians 1:22–23; Colossians 1:18). Based on Paul's statement regarding the "one baptism" in Ephesians 4:4–5, we would conclude that the water rite is not a part of God's program for the Dispensation of Grace. It is not only unnecessary, but it is also inappropriate to practice today under the Dispensation of the Grace of God. Note that Paul's commission to be the apostle of the Gentiles didn't include water baptism (1 Corinthians 1:17), while the commission given to the twelve did (Matt. 28:20; Mark 16:16). In the early part of his ministry as the apostle of the Gentiles, he baptized some with water (1 Corinthians 1:14–16). In the same epistle of 1Corinthians, he also proclaimed a baptism whereby the Holy Spirit joined individual believers to Jesus Christ at the moment of conversion to make that person eternally a member of the body of Christ (1 Corinthians 12:13). In Ephesians 4:5, the apostle says that there is "one baptism." That one baptism for today would be the baptizing work of the Holy Spirit to form the Body of Christ – the church of this present dispensation of grace.

[d] Verses 4–5 speak of our identification with Christ in both His death *and* His resurrection from the dead. This identification of us with Him in His death, burial, *and* resurrection guarantees for us our resurrection. But our resurrection is presented here as a two-fold resurrection. We have a spiritual resurrection now as believers (i.e., "that we also should walk in newness of life") and a physical resurrection later (i.e., "we shall be also in the likeness of his resurrection").

[e] According to 1 Corinthians 15:3–4, the gospel is defined as "Christ died for our sins according to the scriptures; and that he was buried, and that he rose again the third day according to the scriptures." The burial of our Lord was necessary to prove He was indeed dead. For us, His burial (and our burial with Him) presents a demarcation between the life we had before salvation and the life we now have as believers. As a result of that baptism into His death, burial, and resurrection, we can now walk a new walk because we now have and live a new life.

The Old Man Crucified, the Body of Sin Destroyed?

> "⁵ For if we have been planted together in the likeness of his death, we shall be also *in the likeness* of *his* resurrection: ⁶ Knowing this, that our old man[f] is crucified with *him*, that the body of sin[g] might be destroyed, that henceforth we should not serve[h] sin." (Romans 6:5–6)

[f] Here, in Verse 6, the apostle again uses a figure of speech to refer to the person we were before conversion as "our old man." Verse 6 tells us that that person was crucified. He or she was crucified with Christ. It was the baptism of Verse 3 that resulted in our old man being crucified along with (together with) Christ. So let's ask two important questions here:

1. The first question being: Who is our "old man"?

2. The second question: What is the significance of him being crucified?

The answer to each is profound:

1. Our old man is the person we were before conversion when the old Adamic sin nature reigned in our lives and in fact owned our physical bodies.

2. The significance of him being crucified (as indeed he was for the believer) is that the old man no longer exists. We will see in Chapter 7 that the old sin nature still resides in our physical bodies, but the person we were under his rulership no longer exists. We as believers are each a new creature because we are a part of a new creation (a new creature as Paul states it in 2Cor. 5:17).

[g] The term "the body of sin" is also a figure of speech. We ask ourselves two questions regarding this body of sin:

1. What is the body of sin?

2. In what sense was it destroyed when we trusted Jesus Christ?

Here, too, the answers to these questions teach profound truth on the life-changing work of grace:

1. The term "the body of sin" is in the genitive case, indicating in this case possession. The body of sin in this case is the body every believer has now as a saved person but refers to its state before conversion to Christ when the old sin nature still owned it.

2. When we were baptized into His death, burial, and resurrection, our old man was thereby crucified. The ownership of our body by the sin nature ceased, and in that sense it was "destroyed" as "the body of sin." (i.e., it is no longer the body Mr. Sin owns). As believers, our bodies are now under new ownership, that being of Christ (1Corinthians 6:15-17).

[h] God's purpose in baptizing us into Christ's death is that we henceforth do not have to serve sin. Paul was using the figure of speech of personification, in which he was treating the sin nature that still dwells in our physical bodies as if it were a person trying to control us. As I teach this chapter of scripture, I put a title on sin for illustration purposes. I call him "Mr. Sin" to convey the concept that the sin nature once controlled us, lost that control, and is trying to gain it back. To get the impact of this, read Romans Chapters 5 through 7, and whenever "sin" is used as a noun, mentally put the title "Mr." in front of it to convey the impact of the doctrine the apostle taught regarding how we have victory over him through Christ. It is truly the working of God's grace that results in our being set free from the dominion of "Mr. Sin."

Dead unto Sin; Alive unto God

"[7] For he that is dead is freed[i] from sin. [8] Now if we be dead with Christ, we believe that we shall also live[j] with him: [9] Knowing that Christ being raised from the dead dieth no more; death hath no more dominion over him. [10] For in that he died, he died[k] unto sin once: but in that he liveth, he liveth unto God. [11] Likewise reckon[l] ye also yourselves to be dead indeed unto sin, but alive unto God through Jesus Christ our Lord. [12] Let not sin therefore reign[m] in your mortal body, that ye should obey it in the lusts thereof. [13] Neither yield[o] ye your members *as* instruments of unrighteousness unto sin: but yield yourselves unto God, as those that are alive from the dead, and your members *as* instruments of righteousness unto God. [14] For sin shall not have dominion[n] over you: for ye are not[o] under the law, but under grace." (Romans 6:7–14)

[i] "He that is dead is freed from sin" (Verse 7). Not only is my old man (the person I was) crucified, but I am also dead to sin (dead to Mr. Sin).. Death is separation from someone or something. Physical death is separation of the soul and spirit from the physical body (Genesis 35:18). So also "the world is crucified unto me, and I unto the world" (Galatians 6:14). Also, I was once a child of the devil (Ephesians 2:2; Matthew 13:38; John 8:8), but I am now a child of God by that baptism of which Verse 3 speaks.

[j] The doctrine of deliverance from the power, the reign, and the dominion of sin (the old Adamic nature) is given in Romans 6:1–6. The means by which it is appropriated is in Verses 7-14. There are three actions needed to appropriate the victory of that deliverance:

1. Believe that our baptism into Christ's death delivers us from both the penalty and power of sin and made us alive unto God. (Verses 8-10)

2. Reckon it to be a fact that we are indeed dead unto sin but alive unto God through Christ. (Verses 11-12)

3. Refuse to yield the use of the members of our bodies to the old sin nature (i.e. to old Mr. Sin) but rather yield ourselves unto God as those who are alive from the dead to yield our members as instruments of righteousness unto God (Verses 13–14). This is a moment by moment, occasion by occasion decision that we make as believers to appropriate victory over sin.

[k] The Lord Jesus Christ died unto sin once (Verse 10). You can pay the death penalty only once. The significance for the believer is that there was one life surrendered -- that of the old man. So there is now one life to live -- that being the life of Christ. The life that Jesus lives now He is living unto God, and we share that life with Him (cf. Galatians 2:20). In other words, we are living that life of spiritual resurrection with Him now.

[l] Verse 11 talks about us reckoning ourselves to be dead indeed to sin and also reckoning ourselves to be alive unto God. To "reckon" means to make a faith application of something we know to be true in our lives. To "reckon" is to come to a logical conclusion on a matter. That is, we need to see ourselves as God sees us. He sees us as being just as fit for heaven as His only begotten Son is (2 Corinthians 5:21). We are called to live as adult children of God in His family and to engage ourselves in the soul-saving business with our heavenly Father.

[m] The verb rendered "let not reign" in Verse 12 is in the present tense and imperative mode. This speaks of continuous action. The instruction essentially is, "Do not allow Mr. Sin to be continually reigning in your mortal body." The fact that the reference is to the mortal body means this is instruction for the here and now. The instruction is "Do not allow him to run your life." So also the verb *yield* in Verse 13 is also in the present tense and imperative mode. Mr. Sin's power over you as a believer and your body was truly broken by the baptizing work of the Holy Spirit to baptize you into an eternal, living relationship with Jesus Christ. The sin nature cannot do anything any longer in your life unless you allow him to use the members of your body to do so. His power over you has been broken. His ownership over your body has ended. To have victory over him, one has to simply reckon it to be a fact that his power over the believer is indeed broken.

[n] Here in Verse 14, the apostle presents the reason for the injunction of Verse 13. Believers should yield themselves unto God and their members as instruments of righteousness rather than yielding their members to the indwelling sin nature for him (Mr. Sin) to use as instruments of unrighteousness. Believers are not under the dominion of the old sin nature; they are therefore free to choose between the two since they are not bound to follow the old man who was crucified. While a man was yet an unbeliever, the only nature he had was the old sin nature, and it (the sin nature) therefore ran his life (i.e., sin had dominion over him).

[o] Due to the fact that the believer is under grace and not under law, he or she is freed from sin. This is the theme of the rest of this chapter and all of Chapter 7 od Romans. For the believer, being put under law would again give sin (the old sin nature) dominion over him or her again. Chapter 7 will go on to explain why that would be so.

A Form of Doctrine That Delivers from Sin – an Expose of Romans 6:15–23

"[15] What[p] then? Shall[q] we sin, because we are not under the law, but under grace? God forbid. [16] Know ye not, that to whom ye yield[r] yourselves servants to obey, his servants ye are to whom ye obey; whether of sin unto death, or of obedience unto righteousness? [17] But God be thanked, that ye were[s] the servants of sin, but ye have obeyed[t] from the heart that form of doctrine which was delivered you. [18] Being then made[u] free from sin, ye became the servants of righteousness. [19] I speak after the manner of men because of the infirmity of your flesh: for as ye have yielded your members servants to uncleanness and to iniquity unto iniquity; even so now yield your members servants to righteousness unto holiness. [20] For when ye were the servants of sin, ye were free from righteousness. [21] What fruit had ye then in those things whereof ye are now ashamed? for the end of those things *is* death. [22] But now being made[u] free from sin, and become[v] servants to God, ye have your fruit unto holiness, and the end everlasting life. ²³ For the wages[w] of sin *is* death; but the gift of God *is* eternal life through Jesus Christ our Lord." (Romans 6:15–23)

[p] This rhetorical question (Verse 15) is almost identical to that of Verse 1. However, here in Verse 15, "sin" is a verb and denotes the act of sinning, while in Verse 1, "sin" was a noun and denotes the old sin nature. Paul answers the first question (Verse 1) by pointing out that we are dead to sin by our baptism into Christ's death, burial, and resurrection. He answers the second by pointing out that serving sin brings to the believer a functional death that consists of the believer not experiencing victory in his life. However, serving righteousness brings eternal reward to the believer.

[q] The structure of Paul's answers to the rhetorical questions of Verses 1 and 15 is the same. He first gives the simple but emphatic answer: "God forbid." Then he gives the reason for his answer. Whereas the believer is dead to sin and no longer under the dominion of the sin nature, Verses 15–23 state that the believer can still serve the sin nature. The believer has a choice the unbeliever doesn't have. The believer can either serve "sin," the old sin nature or he can serve "obedience," a synonym for the new nature. The "know ye not" is Paul's way of introducing a fundamental truth, as in Verse 3. Here the fundamental truth is that believers have the choice of whom they will serve. They can either serve the sin nature, whose power has been broken (Verse 6), or serve Christ, here referred to as "obedience."

[r] Service to "sin" (the old Adamic sin nature) results in death. This death is neither physical death nor the spiritual death Adam died when he sinned. Rather, this death is best understood as spiritual dormancy (or a functional death), as Romans 8:13 states. "For if ye live after the flesh, ye shall die: but if ye through the Spirit do mortify the deeds of the body, ye shall live." Rather than serving sin, the believer is admonished to serve "obedience" (the new man who exhibited "the obedience of faith" in getting justified) with the end result being righteousness -- righteousness in practice.

[s] "Ye were the servants of sin" (Verse 17). This takes us back to the time before we came in faith to the Savior, back in our individual lives before we were baptized into Christ's death to render our old man "crucified" (Romans 6:6). At that time our bodies belonged to "sin" (the old man), and therefore we served sin.

[t] The phrase "ye have obeyed from the heart" is an expression for faith in "a form of doctrine." That "form of doctrine" is found back in Romans 3:21–28 and 6:1-4 regarding the cross and what was accomplished there. See Romans 1:5, especially Romans 16:26, on how this term is used elsewhere.

[u] The believer was "made free from sin" (i.e., set at liberty from it) by believing the form of doctrine that resulted in him or her being justified. When my old man was crucified with Christ, the body of sin was no longer the body the sin nature owned, and I was set free from him.

[v] The physical body of the believer, as is his or her soul and spirit (1Corinthians 6:19–20), is now owned by Jesus Christ to form the new creature of 2Corinthians 5:17 ("Therefore if any man be in Christ, he is a new creature: old things are passed away; behold, all things are become new"). Now then, as one who has been delivered from the bondage of sin, the believer is now a servant to what is here called "righteousness." This term is yet another name for the new nature. Note in Verse 22 that, when the believer became a servant to righteousness, he or she became a servant to God. Later in Romans, other names are added. The sin nature is called "the flesh" in Romans 8:1. The new man is called "the Spirit of Christ" in Romans 8:9. Each of the two natures, the sin nature and the Spirit of Christ, will produce fruit. We don't gather grapes from a thorn bush (Matthew 7:16). The end result of the fruit the old sin nature produces is death. On the other hand, the fruit the new nature produces in the believer is holiness. This fruit will abide forever, and the believer will enjoy that fruit that the Spirit of Christ bears in the eternal life the believer has.

[w] Not surprisingly, Mr. Sin pays wages. The wages he pays is death. Romans 6:23 says wages are the recompense for work, while a gift is bestowed by grace. This takes us to the concept of the *works* of the flesh versus the *fruit* of the Spirit in Galatians 5:19–23. Sin (the old nature) pays wages, those being death. The death is spiritual death, resulting in the second death in the lake of fire in the unsaved man or death as far as one's Christian experience is concerned in the saved man. The gift of God, however, is eternal life. This life is the resurrection life given to every believer (both spiritual resurrection as in Philippians 3:11 and physical, bodily resurrection as in 1 Corinthians 15:51).

CHAPTER 5
DEALING WITH LIFE IN THE TWENTY-FIRST CENTURY

How to live successfully in perilous times

An Expose of 2Timothy Chapter 3 on the Last Days: The apostle Paul describes the last days of the dispensation of grace as "Perilous times" in this passage. We are living in those perilous times now. We therefore need to know how to be properly adjusted to these times and how to prosper spiritually in them. The apostle gives us advice on this in the following passage:

2 Timothy 3:1-17 "[a]1 This know also, that in the last days[b] perilous times shall come. 2 For men shall be[c] lovers of their own selves, covetous, boasters, proud, blasphemers, disobedient to parents, unthankful, unholy, 3 Without natural affection, trucebreakers, false accusers, incontinent, fierce, despisers of those that are good, 4 Traitors, heady, highminded, lovers of pleasures more than lovers of God; 5 Having a form[d] of godliness, but denying[e] the power[f] thereof: from such[g] turn[h] away. 6 For of this sort are they which creep into houses, and lead[i] captive silly women laden with sins, led away with divers lusts, 7 Ever learning, and never able[j] to come to the knowledge[k] of the truth. 8 Now[l] as Jannes and Jambres withstood Moses, so do these also resist the truth: men of corrupt minds, reprobate concerning the faith. 9 But[m] they shall proceed no further: for their folly shall be manifest unto all *men*, as theirs also was.

10 But thou hast fully known[n] my doctrine, manner of life, purpose, faith, longsuffering, charity, patience, 11 Persecutions, afflictions, which came unto me at Antioch, at Iconium, at Lystra; what persecutions I [o] endured: but out of *them* all the Lord delivered me. 12 Yea, and all that will[p] live godly in Christ Jesus shall suffer persecution. 13 But evil[q] men and seducers shall wax worse and worse, deceiving, and being deceived. 14 But continue[r] thou in the things which thou hast learned and hast been assured of, knowing of whom thou hast learned *them*; 15 And that from[s] a child thou hast known the holy scriptures, which are able to make thee wise unto salvation through faith which is in Christ Jesus. 16 All scripture[t] *is* given by inspiration of God, and *is* profitable for doctrine, for reproof, for correction, for instruction in righteousness: 17 That the man of God may be perfect, throughly furnished unto all good works."

Let's study this passage:

[a] While 1Timothy 4:1-3 concerns apostasy in the professing church during the present dispensation, 2Timothy 3:1-7 concerns conditions in the world during this same time. In 1Timothy 4 we see that "some shall depart from the faith" while here we see that "perilous times shall come." The reason for those times becoming ever more perilous

with time is the active intervention of Satan in the course of human events. He is today the "spirit that now worketh in the children of disobedience" (Eph. 2:2). He is also "the god of this world." (2Cor. 4:4) Now with the advent of radio and television and the internet, Satan's world and his influence has a direct pipeline into the homes of saved and unsaved alike. The trend presented here is evident in all "men" – saved and unsaved alike.

[b] The "Last days" of Paul are not the same days as the last days of prophecy as referred to in Daniel, Matthew, and the Revelation. The last days of Paul have a reference to the last days of the Dispensation of the Grace of God – the days just prior to the rapture (the catching away) of the church to its home in heaven. The last days of prophecy, however, have reference to the last days just prior to and including the return of Christ to the earth to end "the times of the Gentiles."

[c] The character of mankind in the last days of the dispensation of grace in general shall be:

- "Lovers of their own selves". The prevalent philosophies of our day focuses on self and exalt the individual. We live in a "Selfie World" today. The formula for success is said to be "being sold on yourself." Contentment is said to be the ability to "accept yourself." Rather than identifying the source of sin as the indwelling sin nature, evil and wicked acts are blamed on an individual's lack of "self esteem." But "The Lord is nigh unto them that are of a broken heart, and saveth such as be of a contrite spirit" (Psalm 34:18). Job understood this when he said before the Lord, "I abhor myself, and repent in dust and ashes" (Job 42:6). *See also Isaiah 57:15; 66:2; Romans 7:18, 24, and 25.*

- "Covetous". This is the word used of the Pharisees in Luke 16:14. The affluence of modern society has produced a disdain for austerity and a love for the things that make for a comfortable life. The desire for material wealth is here in view. Such desire shapes the character of a society that is preoccupied with it. Timothy was warned to flee from this in 1Timothy 6:10-11.

- "Boasters" (empty pretenders). This is the lack of modesty that we see prevalent throughout our society. It is the attitude that says "I can and I will" without credit to God who has the real ability. This "self confidence" ought not be the attitude of the Spirit-led believer, for "our sufficiency is of Christ" (2Cor. 2:16 *cf* Phil 3:3-9; Proverbs 14:26; Psalm 118:8-9).

- "Proud" (literally "to show above"). This is the person who holds himself to be above others and looks down on them. It is the arrogance that characterizes essentially all of the entertainment industry and much of the political, educational, and even ecclesiastical elements of our society today. This is the haughty spirit that God abhors (2Sam. 22:28; Prov. 21:24) and which will be judged (Prov. 16:18; Isa. 10:33).

- "Blasphemer" (slanderous, reproachful, and abusive in behavior). Particularly verbal behavior. The name of Jesus Christ and of God are blasphemed by men who spurn the grace that could save them from the judgment of the one they blaspheme (Rev 20:11-15).

- "Disobedient to parents". The end result is disobedience of children but the cause is the irresponsibility of parents. That irresponsibility is the outgrowth of a humanistic philosophy which sacrifices loving parental discipline on the altar of so called "human rights" (children's rights here). But, instead of safeguarding the "rights" of children, this philosophy (if and when actually followed) results in frustrated and exasperated parents abusing disobedient and undisciplined children.

- "Unthankful." This speaks of the belief that "the world owes them a living." The social welfare systems of most countries today reinforce this by professing that it does owe them a living. As a result, you rarely find gratitude for kindness shown.

- "Unholy" -- a negative attitude toward God, His Word, and His will.

- "Without natural affections," natural affections being that of parents toward children and vice versa, or that of a spouse toward one's mate. This is the cementing agent that God provided to hold any social unit (e.g. the family) together.

- "Trucebreakers." It means literally to refuse to be reconciled. The word is translated "implacable" in Romans 1:31. It could refer as well to one to whom a truce or reconciliation means nothing.

- "False accusers." Here the thought is that of a false accusation that is thrown between friends with the idea of breaking friendships (Proverbs 16:28-29).

- "Incontinent," meaning "powerless." The idea is to be powerless in control over self; to lack self control. It is to give free reign to the promptings of the depraved mind without regard to the welfare of self or others. This is the characteristic of modern man that makes our streets unsafe to traverse without a bodyguard.

- "Fierce" (untamed). It has the idea of being brutal and savage. This is a prevalent theme in the entertainment medias.

- "Despisers of those that are good;" good meaning true, honorable, just, pure, lovely, and / or of good report, as in Philippians 4:8. One would think that a good person would be appreciated but that will not be the norm in the last days.

- "Traitors", one who betrays a trust for personal gain. The word is used in Luke 6:16 and Acts 7:52 of those who betrayed Christ.

- "Heady," to go headlong into evil with a reckless disregard for consequence. It describes a person who is headstrong and reckless.

- "High minded" (literally "to raise a smoke"), to be puffed up with pride to the point where one becomes an airhead. These are people who think more highly of themselves than they ought to think (Rom. 12:3).

- "Lovers of pleasure more than lovers of God." That men today love pleasure is self evident -- simply tune in to the sporting events, music concerts, movies, etc. and note the self centered (as opposed to God centered) thrust of it all. The word "more" here is not referring to degree but means "rather than." Pleasure becomes the god that is put up in place of the true God.

[d] This passage (2Tim. 3:1-6) has the state of the world in the last days of the Dispensation of the Grace of God in view, while 1Timothy 4:1-9 has the state of the professing church in view. Here we see the world "having a form of

godliness." "Having" carries the idea of holding, or possessing. Note that it is *a* form of godliness that they possess and not *the* form. In 1Timothy 6:5 some were teaching gain as a means of godliness and that gain is a measure of godliness. Here we see that there exists an empty form that is passed off as godliness. This has reference to the hollow religious rites, rituals, and ecclesiastical systems that are presented as godliness but are in reality filled with humanistic thinking, secular psychology and just simply show and entertainment.

[e] "Denying the power thereof..." here means to disown, disclaim, or renounce in the passive voice. The passive voice implies that they were denied the power of God. We ask "Who could have denied them the power of godliness?" Obviously it was Satan who blinds the mind of them that believe not (2Cor. 4:4) and who now works in the children of disobedience (Eph. 2:2). The present result is a state of mental blindness to the power of true godliness.

[f] Though religion can put on a good show, it cannot produce in its adherents any real power. The "power" here in Verse 5 is the ability to make real and permanent positive changes in peoples' lives. This can come only by the Spirit of God working by grace through faith (the believer's faith) in the yielded heart of the genuine believer. It is not something that can be produced in the strength of the flesh. This is what Paul was looking for when he told the Corinthians, "I...will know, not the speech of them which are puffed up, but the power" (1Cor. 4:19). Paul appreciated being taught this lesson as he says, "Most gladly therefore will I rather glory in my infirmities, that the power of Christ might rest upon me" (2Cor. 12:9).

[g] "From such" refers to those exhibiting the characteristics of Verses 1-5, but especially Verse 5, "having a form of godliness but denying the power thereof." Appendix 3 addresses what is touted as a modern day phenomena – a character trait labeled "narcissism." Modern day psychology regards it as a personality disorder – a sickness. This so called "personality disorder" embodies much of what we read about in Verses 1-5.To call it a sickness does an injustice to those who are caught up in it in that it gives them and excuse to continue in it. Scripture would call it "sin" and "the flesh." Psychology in general would declare that it is an untreatable condition. However, both sin and the flesh have a cure. That cure is a spiritual one because it is in fact a spiritual issue. The cross is the cure for both sin and the flesh. Regeneration and then a walk in the spirit is the path to recovery from the flesh. The reader is here encouraged to check out Appendix 3 on this pertinent, contemporary subject.

[h] Paul's policy was to avoid head on confrontations with apostates and heretics (Titus 3:10), having given them proper warning. "A man that is an heretic after the first and second admonition reject."

[i] Out of these who are pleasure lovers rather than God lovers in Verse 4, (even though they have a form of godliness but deny the power of real godliness) are those men who use "a form of godliness" to exploit "silly women."

- "Creep into" -- to enter by disguise. They wouldn't have gained entrance had they been honest about their intentions.

- "Lead captive" is to subdue or ensnare. It is used in Luke 21:24, "and they shall be lead away captive into all nations." It means to take captive by use of some force or at least (at first) against their will.

- "Silly women" means literally "little women" -- not in physical stature, but in character. It is used in a contemptuous sense here. These are women who are small in moral character.

- "Laden with" means "heaped upon with". The verb is in the perfect passive indicative. Therefore, they had been heaped upon with sins and are therefore still laden with them. They had been already involved with sins of promiscuity and are now being taken advantage of further by these men.

- "Led away"-They (the silly women) were continually being led away captive.

- "Lusts" is translated "desires" when used in the positive sense, but "lusts" (as it is here) when used in the negative sense. These lusts are the means by which these "little women" were led away captive. They had numerous fleshly and psychological cravings and desires which made them susceptible to the snares of their immoral captors.

[j] The question here is whether "ever learning but never able to come to the knowledge of the truth" applies to the "silly women" taken captive, or to their captors. The answer is that it is true of both. .The learning can come either from teaching or from experience (*cf* Rom 16:17; Phil 4:11). These women were learning from their apostate captors and from their immoral experiences. But, what they were learning was only worldly wisdom, and therefore they are "never able to come to the knowledge of the truth." The same actually applies to their captors as well.

[k] "Never able to come to the knowledge of the truth..." The word translated "Knowledge" is the word for full knowledge. They were ever gaining knowledge, but never gaining full, complete, mature knowledge. "Truth" is a word which has a variety of contexts. In Paul's epistles, though, it has but one meaning -- the revelation given by our Lord from heaven to him for us. Consider the use of the word in the following examples: 1Corinthians 13:8; Galatians. 2:5, 14; Ephesians 1:13; Acts 20:24; and Colossians 1:5. This truth revealed by Christ to him (Gal. 1:12), is also what he refers to as "my gospel" (Rom. 16:25) and "thy mystery" (Eph. 3:2-9). Why were these women unable to come to the knowledge of the truth? 1Timothy 2:12-15 gives us the answer. In spiritual matters, women need genuinely godly men to guide them in spiritual matters. These men are not godly though they display an outward manifestation of godliness. They deny the power of godliness.

[l] "Now" in Verse 8 implies a continuation of the discussion of the character of men in the last days. The apostle uses two Old Testament characters to illustrate the men in the last days by bringing in Jannes and Jambres. This is an example of the law of subsequent narration. This is the first time these two men are named. Their names do not appear in Exodus 7:11-12 where the account is documented. Just as Jannes and Jambres withstood Moses, so will men in the last days resist the truth. They "withstood" in the sense that they stood against or opposed Moses. These men "resist the truth" by taking a continual and unrelenting position against the truth. "Men" here means mankind in general, not simply a male member of the human race. The subjects here were at one point in time corrupted in mind, and they continue in that state. The passive voice implies that they were corrupted in mind (in their reasoning faculties) by someone else. The term "Reprobate concerning the faith" here implies they were presented with the truth but did not accept the correction (Rom. 1:28; Titus 1:16).

[m] "But" is the strong adversative. Though they oppose the truth, they will go only so far before their folly is manifest to all. The mindless nonsense of those who appose the truth becomes evident when the truth is presented as a contrast to the folly of error. It will be clearly evident to all that these men who oppose the truth are operating apart from sound logic. Just as Jannes and Jambres must have looked pretty silly when their snakes were swallowed up by Moses', so will these men look silly when their "form of godliness" is shown to lack real power. Note however,

that those who watched Jannes' and Jambres' folly did not follow Moses even though he evidently had the superior power. So we today can likewise expect that, even though the folly of apostate leaders is self-evident, men will not automatically follow after real godliness. The absurdity of the "Woke" culture of our modern society is a modern example of such folly.

[n] Timothy had "fully known" Paul's ministry having traveled with him (1Cor. 4:17; Phil. 2:19-23). The things in Verse 9 refer to the things of Paul's life style that Timothy fully knew. These ways stand in contrast to the character of men in the last days, as cited in Verses 1-8. These things of Paul and which Timothy had closely followed refer to his:

- "Doctrine" (his teaching) "The glorious gospel of the blessed God, which was committed to my trust" (1Tim. 1:10-11).

  "The doctrine which is according to godliness" (1Tim. 6:3).

  "The time will come when they will not endure sound doctrine" (2Tim. 4:3).

  "Holding fast the faithful word as he hath been taught, that he may be able by sound doctrine both to exhort and to convince the gainsayers" (Titus 1:9).

  "But speak thou the things which become sound doctrine" (Titus 2:1).

  This doctrine is collectively called "the gospel of the grace of God" (Acts 20:24). It contains the information for life in the dispensation of the grace of God (Eph. 3:2) and was committed uniquely to Paul (Col. 1:25-27). It is also called the "revealed mystery" (Rom. 16:25), "the mystery of God" (1Cor. 2:1), "the wisdom of God in a mystery" (1Cor. 2:7), "the Mystery of the Gospel" (Eph. 6:19), "The Word of God, the Mystery" (Col. 1:25-26), and "the mystery of Christ" (Col. 4:3).

- "Manner of life" (on earth)
  Timothy had closely followed Paul's manner of life, having ministered with him for more than fifteen years. They were "equally souled" in this (Phil. 2:20).

- "Purpose"
  God has a purpose -- something that He predetermined to do. That purpose was to call out the Body of Christ from the lost masses of humanity (Rom. 8:28-29; 9:11; Eph. 1:11). Paul (and Timothy) likewise purposed to be workers together with God in this (2Cor. 5:18-21)

- "Faith"
  This characteristic describes one who is fully persuaded of a fact and demonstrates it by his actions. It has the idea of faithfulness (Rom. 3:3; Col. 2:12; Philemon 1:5). Faith (belief) is always the background for faithfulness. True faith spawns faithfulness (Gal. 5:22; 1Tim. 2:15; 4:12).

- "Longsuffering"
  Used by Paul 11 times, this is of prime importance in the life of the believer (Gal. 5:22; Eph. 4:2; Col. 1:11; 3:12-13).

- "Charity" (Love in the sense of liberality freely given to the poor and needy).
  It describes one's readiness even to die for the one so loved (Gal. 2:20; Eph. 5:2, 25).

  This love is not human in origin, nor is it produced by our emotions. It is the love of God poured out in our hearts (Rom. 5:5 cf. 8:35). It is something that flows out of a conscious decision by the believer (Col. 3:19). It abounds in an environment of full knowledge and discernment (Phil. 1:9). It is a love that is a "tough love," even to discipline for the good of the one loved (Heb. 12:6).

- "Patience"
  It is patient endurance of afflictions from unbelievers and sometimes even at the hands of believers. It is produced by and is the result of tribulation (Rom. 5:3). A minister of the gospel was to have much patience (2Cor. 6:4). Timothy was to pursue it (1Tim. 6:11). The effectiveness of a minister of the Word is directly related to his patience.

- "Persecutions"
  The verb form means to pursue as in a hunt. The noun here means to be the one pursued. The pursuit could be to the point of death. The idea is that the one targeted is pursued with the intent of inflicting injury. Paul was so pursued throughout the Book of Acts (e.g. Acts 13:50). Paul had been earlier in life himself a persecutor (Gal. 1:13).

[o] "Afflictions" This speaks of an evil experience or evil treatment. We get our English words "pathetic" and "pathogen" from it. Some of these persecutions and afflictions of Paul are documented for us in Acts 13:44-52 (Antioch), Acts 14:1-6 (Iconium), and Acts 14:8-20 (Lystra). At Lystra, he was possibly stoned to death (2Cor. 12:1-5), and probably was stoned to death according to Leviticus 20:2.

Paul endured these persecutions but the Lord delivered him out of them all. Paul was assured of such deliverance by a personal appearance of our Lord (Acts 18:9-10). Paul requested prayers for further deliverance (Rom. 15:31 and 2Thess. 3:2). There is as much need for prayer today (for believers to pray for each other for deliverance) as there was then. In fact, today it is even more imperative because "evil men and seducers shall wax worse and worse" (Verse 13).

[p] The words "All that will" in Verse 12 is the present nominative participle meaning literally "those who are willing." The all here is limited by "that will" or all that are willing to and therefore resolve to live godly. Remember that in the last days men will be "despisers of them that are good." So too, the message of those who will live godly is not a popular message in that:

> It condemns all other belief systems as untrue and dangerous.
> It mortifies self and its passions.
> It teaches doctrines that are hard to believe (the resurrection of the dead as an example).

Godliness is something that can only be produced in the believer and produced only as he/she walks "after the Spirit" (Rom. 8:4, 12-14). It is driven by the working of the new man and is therefore dependent on the knowledge of the doctrine concerning the new man (Rom 6:1-10). It is operative in the believer by a faith response to that doctrine (Rom. 6:11-23). Godliness is that natural result of being "filled with the Spirit" (Eph. 5:18-20).

All that "will live godly" (i.e. all that make a resolve to live godly) shall suffer persecution. "Shall suffer persecution" is in the future passive indicative. It means that they will be pursued with the intent of being persecuted. Persecution begins as soon as one "intends" to live godly and continues against those who stay the course and indeed do live godly (2Cor. 4:9; Gal. 4:29). The believer's response to persecution is then to "...bless them that persecute you" (Rom. 12:14). In fact, we believers are to labor on behalf of those who persecute us (1Cor. 4:9) that we might reach them with the gospel.

[q] In Verse 13 the apostle sets evil men and seducers in contrast with those who will live godly. The word for "Evil" in this form is the same word used to describe the man living in an incestuous relationship in 1Corinthians 5:13. In Colossians 1:21 it describes the wicked works of unbelievers. In Matthew 13:19 it is used in reference to the devil. Here, it includes women and children, as "those who use deceit." These evil men and seducers "Shall wax worse and worse." So much for the notion that the church will bring in the millennium. The word "wax," as translated, means "proceed." The word "worse" is a comparative term. Evil men in the last days shall be more evil than in Paul's day. Seducers likewise will be more deceitful.

The seducers will not only deceive others but they themselves will be deceived. These men will be deceived both by each other and by Satan (2Cor. 4:4; Eph. 2:2; Titus 3:3). These men are in a vicious circle of deception (Rom. 1:21, 24, 26, and 28).

[r] So what is the believer to do in the face of such deception? In the midst of the perils of the last days, the believer is not left without a guide and a safeguard from deception. The saints in the last days (as all saints did) would have the Word of God as a guide to keep from being misled. "The things which thou hast learned" in Verse 14 is "that which was committed to thy trust" (1Tim. 6:20). It is "that good thing which was committed unto thee" and which Timothy was to "keep by the Holy Ghost which dwelleth in us" (1Tim. 1:14). If Timothy would continue in these things, he would be set in contrast to the evil men and seducers who would wax worse and worse. By so doing, he could stand against the evil men around him no matter how great their numbers or how fierce their attack might be (Rom. 15:1; Eph. 6:11-14). "Of whom thou hast learned them" here in Verse 14 suggests that others are associated with Paul in the communication of truth to Timothy (2Tim. 2:2). In light of all that Paul says in his epistles, however, it is clear that what Timothy had learned, he received from Paul (1Tim. 1:3; 6:6, 11; 6:2; 2Tim. 1:13-14; 3:10). The source of this truth was Jesus Christ. The Lord revealed it to Paul who then taught it to Timothy in conjunction with others (Gal. 1:12; Col. 1:24-28).

Timothy had learned and had been assured of those things. "Learned" here speaks of knowledge gained by both observation and listening. Paul states in Philippians 4:9 that what he did and taught were to be a pattern for all believers. God grant that every man of God would do the same. "And hast been assured of in one self" means to be totally convinced of a message so that one acts according to it. Timothy was solid and steadfast in the message that he had received from Paul.

[s] "And" could mean "and", "even", or "also." Here, in 2Timothy3:15, the context dictates that we understand a somewhat different thought being introduced. While Verse 14 speaks of what Timothy learned from Paul, Verse 15 speaks of what Timothy learned from his mother and grandmother. This is a powerful statement that the total lifestyle of the mother is impressed upon the infant. The child learns the scripture from the mother by language but the application of it by actions. "The holy scriptures" is the writings that are sacred -- uniquely God's. "Able" here in Verse 15 refers to the Holy Scriptures' power to do work in people's lives.

The scriptures which Paul has reference to are the Old Testament Scriptures. Here in Verse 15, they are seen as making Timothy "wise unto salvation through faith which is in Christ Jesus". Neither Eunice (Timothy's mother) nor Lois (his grandmother) knew anything about the "salvation through faith which in Christ Jesus" until Paul and Barnabas came to Lystra (Acts 16:1-3). The point that Paul is making, however, is that the Old Testament Scriptures have the ability to give insight into the person of Christ. The scriptures (both Old & New Testament) form one whole unit. Having faith in the Old Testament Scriptures, Timothy carried that confidence to the writings of Paul which are likewise scripture of equal authority.

[t] "All scripture" -- If it is scripture, it is given by inspiration of God. The word "Scripture" refers to scripture in general. All of it is "Given by inspiration of God" -- literally it was God breathed. If it is scripture, it came directly from the mouth of God just as your words come out of your mouth. It was not the men who wrote it that were inspired, but rather the scripture (the writings themselves) that were inspired. In 2Peter 1:21 we see a powerful statement of inspiration in that "holy men of God spake as they were moved by the Holy Ghost." The term "moved" is a nautical term that speaks of a sailing vessel "being borne along" by the action of the wind in the sails. The men who wrote the words were more the pen than the pen man. The Holy Spirit was the real pen man.

An interesting footnote on the canonicity of Paul's epistles is found in 2Peter 3:16. There we see Peter's statement that people will twist things in Paul's epistles as they do the "other scriptures." In Romans 16:25, Paul's message was revealed by scriptures prophetic. These scriptures refer to his own writings, which were identified as scripture by the New Testament prophets (Acts 15:32).

All scripture is profitable for four things:

1. Teaching -- that which is taught (I Tim. 1:10, 11; 4:6; II Tim/ 2:2; cf Phil. 4:9).

2. Reproof -- to convince of wrong doing (Rom. 8:13-16; Col. 1:9-10).

3. Correction -- to straighten up or upon (Col. 3:10; Eph. 4:23-24). Scripture is profitable for restoring a man to what God would have him to be.

4. Instruction in righteousness -- educating and disciplining children in that which is right (Eph. 6:4).

"The man of God"- The only other usage of this phrase is in 1Timothy 6:11. Is this term to be understood as applying only to Timothy, only to preachers, or is it to apply to every believer? It seems clear from Romans 6:10-13 that God wants every believer to be uniquely God's. The translation of "perfect" means "completely" or "thoroughly furnished." It is a maritime term used to describe a ship that is fully filled, manned, loaded, stocked, and with all papers in order for a long voyage. "Unto all good works" – the scripture fully equips the believer to do everything that God would have him do (1Cor. 15:58; 2Cor. 9:8; Titus 3:8, 14; 1Tim. 6:18; Titus 2:14; Eph. 2:10; etc.).

A Lesson on Parenting from the Rechabites:

The material in the following four pages is an excerpt from the book *You and Your Creator* (Tiry 2019). I include it here because it is particularly relevant for parenting in these last days of the Dispensation of Grace.

I enjoy the lesson that the Lord taught Israel through Jeremiah the prophet in Jeremiah Chapter 35. It tells us volumes about how to maintain personal godliness in a nation that was in spiritual decline. Israel was on the verge of moral collapse because of their failure in parenting.

The prophet Jeremiah is often called the weeping prophet. As we read the book of Jeremiah we find that it strikes a familiar chord in our hearts regarding our society today. God, speaking through Jeremiah says *"The sin of Judah is written with a pen of iron and with the point of a diamond: it is graven upon the table of their heart, and upon the horns of your altars; Whilst their children remember their altars and their groves by the green trees upon the high hills."* (Jeremiah 17:1&2) What a sad state -- the parents were living a licentious life style and the children departed from the LORD.

As we look out across the present moral landscape of the USA, we can imagine God speaking such a manner of us and of our society as we enter the 21st century. We can dismiss it as the actions and attitudes of the unsaved masses. But the problem is that believers in increasing numbers find that their children are picking up those decadent actions and attitudes.

In my experiences in ministering the gospel to people over the years, people have asked time and again "What can we do for our children to stem the tide of worldliness?" Else they ask "Is it possible to bring up children in this world so that they not be conformed to the world?" In response to those questions, I often recount the case of the Rechabites.

So "Who are the Rechabites?" you ask. They were a most fascinating family of people in Israel. The Lord used the Rechabites to teach Jeremiah an important lesson on why the nation was on the moral state they were in. It was through Jeremiah that the Lord announced that Israel would be taken captive in Babylon for 70 years (2Chronicles 36:21; Daniel 9:2; Jeremiah 26:6 & 7) because of their sin and worldly attitudes. Now the Lord was going to give Israel an object lesson through Jeremiah as to the reason for their decadent state that led to their captivity. It is a most interesting object lesson.

In Jeremiah 35:2 the LORD tells Jeremiah *"Go unto the house of the Rechabites, and speak unto them, and bring them into the house of the LORD, into one of the chambers, and give them wine to drink."* So Jeremiah did as the Lord commanded (Jeremiah 35:5-8) *"And I set before the sons of the house of the Rechabites pots full of wine, and cups, and I said unto them, Drink ye wine. But they said, We will drink no wine: for Jonadab the son of Rechab our father commanded us, saying, Ye shall drink no wine, neither ye, nor your sons for ever: Neither shall ye build house, nor sow seed, nor plant vineyard, nor have any: but all your days ye shall dwell in tents: that ye may live many days in the land where ye be strangers. Thus have we obeyed the voice of Jonadab the son of Rechab our father in all that he hath charged us, to drink no wine all our days, we, our wives, our sons, nor our daughters".*

Now just so we do not miss the point, it was not against the Law of Moses to drink wine in Israel. Nor was it wrong to build houses or plant vineyards. The point that the LORD wanted Jeremiah to catch and to tell to Israel had to do with the successful communicating of Bible doctrine from generation to generation to generation to .... We see this point as the Lord speaks to Jeremiah *"Then came the word of the Lord unto Jeremiah saying, Thus saith the Lord of hosts, the God of Israel; Go and tell the men of Juda and the inhabitants of Jerusalem. Will ye not receive instruction to hearken to my words? Saith the LORD. The words of Jonadab the son of Rechab, that he commanded his sons not to drink wine, are performed; for unto this day they drink none, but obey their father's commandment: notwithstanding I have spoken unto you, rising early and speaking; but ye hearkened not unto me"* (Jeremiah 35:12-14).

The interesting thing about this incident is that it occurred about 600 B.C. We have to go back in time to about 880 B.C. (280 years earlier) to find Jehonadab (same person) the son of Rechab. We find him in 2Kings 10:15 where he is in league with Jehu as they purge the prophets of Baal from Israel. Jehonadab was clearly a man with a great zeal for the Lord. It was a zeal that he was readily able to communicate on to his children and his children to their children. Such is the enduring legacy of a godly father. And the pattern continued for some 10 plus generations when Jeremiah meets this godly family.

To get a proper perspective on this important lesson for us relative to the subject of parenting, let's consider that Israel was in a state of moral decay and spiritual darkness but they were not always that way. There were times in Israel's history when they were truly focused on the LORD. They were so when Joshua led them over Jordan to enter the Promised Land. They were again as the LORD led them to great victories over their enemies under the reign of David the King. But those were years that were long gone by. They were now as a nation, at the point where all they could look forward to was seventy years of captivity in Babylon. Had the entire nation been able to have a real zeal for the LORD and to communicate that zeal to succeeding generations, the nation would not be facing this pending and sure chastening of the LORD.

We ask then the question, "Is success in parenting just the luck of the draw and a simple matter of happenstance? Or is success in parenting a skill that can be learned from a father and communicated unto the children?" If it were just a matter of happenstance, the LORD's object lesson to Jeremiah would be pointless. Rather, the truth of Proverbs 22:6 *"Train up a child in the way he should go: and when he is old, he will not depart from it"* remains a fact. This is a fact that Satan and his henchmen know far better than believers seem to. Vladimir Lenin said "Give me four years to teach the children and the seed I have sown will never be uprooted." A saying of the Jesuits is "Give me a child for the first seven years, and you may do what you like with him afterwards." Oh, how important those first years of a child's life is in the communication of the things of the Lord and things that form character.

So let's ask again "Is it possible to raise godly kids?" The answer that we get from Scripture is Yes! We find this clearly presented in 1Timothy 3: 4 & 12 where the apostle states the qualifications of elders and deacons. An elder must be *"One that ruleth well his own house, having his children in subjection with all gravity; (For if a man know not how to rule his own house, how shall he take care of the church of God?)"* And again *"Let the deacons be the husbands of one wife, ruling their children and their own houses well."* Obviously, godly husbandry and parenting is a skill that can be learned and conveyed, as any other skill can be. And, as we consider the consequences, it is the most important skill that we parents (and especially husbands and fathers) need to master.

So what does it take to be successful in parenting?

Zeal for the Truth - It takes first of all a zeal for the Lord. Let's revisit Jehonadab the godly father of that long line of godly fathers. We find him in 2 Kings 10:23-25 purging out the prophets of Baal and destroying the idolatrous images from Israel. He had zeal for the LORD and for his nation to restore his nation to the LORD. Such zeal is contagious.

A Genuine Heart of Love - It takes a love that compels a man to set aside all other interest but that of the eternal spiritual welfare of those precious lives that have been committed to his trust. Our example of such love is our Lord

Himself *"Husbands love your wives, even as Christ also loved the church, and gave himself for it. That he might sanctify and cleanse it with the washing of water the word..."* With regard to those children, fathers are instructed by the apostle to love their children with a love that seeks first and foremost to bring them up in the nurture and admonition of the Lord (Ephesians 6:4). If every Christian father would look at that newborn offspring of his and have a real appreciation for the marvel and the wonder of it all and realize that where and how that child spends eternity is largely dependent upon him and what he does in the next 18 years, the state of the Christian home in America would be far better.

It Takes Authority – It takes authority to bring up a child in the nurture and admonition of the Lord. Modern society has been working fervently for the last 50 years to convince parents that they do not have authority. If there be one factor that has produced the undisciplined, disrespectful, and generally rude and obnoxious behavior of many of the American teens today it is the lack of respect for authority. Oh how we need husbands and fathers who understand that they need to exercise their God given authority in the home to be aggressively benevolent on behalf of their charges in the matter of the nurture and admonition of the Lord.

It takes spiritual maturity. All of us start in the Christian life as babes in Christ. However, God does not expect us to be babes very long. *"As newborn babes, desire the sincere [pure] milk of the word, that ye may grow thereby:"* (1Peter: 2:2). But God would have us all come to maturity so as to handle the meat fit for the spiritual appetite of the mature saint. The apostle defines for us the real meat of scripture in 1Corinthians 2:6-8 *"Howbeit we speak wisdom among them that are perfect: [mature] yet not the wisdom of this world, nor of the princes of this world, that come to nought: But we speak the wisdom of God in a mystery, even the hidden wisdom, which God ordained before the world unto our glory: Which none of the princes of this world knew: for had they known it, they would not have crucified the Lord of glory"*. It takes a mature saint to understand the preaching of Jesus Christ according to the revelation of the mystery and to live that doctrine out in his life. As a man studies the Word rightly divided and humbly (and indeed it must be humbly) applies it to his life, he develops "the mind of Christ" (1Corinthians 2:15). Having the mind of Christ, he sees the world as Christ sees the world. He sees his family as Christ sees them. He loves them as Christ loves them. Most importantly He sacrifices for them as Christ sacrificed for His church (Ephesians 5:25)

It takes a disciplined life. As in the matter of reaping what is sown, it takes a disciplined life to reproduce a disciplined life. The word "discipline" comes from the word disciple. We as parents ought to think of disciplining our children as to disciple them. That is, to make disciples of them. Success in parenting is not achieved until we as parents are standing shoulder to shoulder with our children as disciples of the Lord with all (the parents and children) receiving instruction from Christ (the living Word) through the Bible (the written Word).

It takes a strategy for success. It has been well said that if you aim at nothing you will hit it every time. We have as believers a target to aim at. It is stated for us in Ephesians 4:13-16

> "13: Till we all come in the unity of the faith, and of the knowledge of the Son of God, unto a perfect man, unto the measure of the stature of the fulness of Christ: 14: That we henceforth be no more children, tossed to and fro, and carried about with every wind of doctrine, by the sleight of men, and cunning craftiness, whereby they lie in wait to deceive; 15: But speaking the truth in love, may grow up into him in all things, which is the head, even Christ: 16: From whom the whole body fitly joined together and compacted by that which every joint supplieth, according to the effectual working in the measure of every part, maketh increase of the body unto the edifying of itself in love."

The strategy for success in our lives and that of our families is to realize that we as believers have a three-fold enemy of the world, the flesh, and the devil. The strategy for defending ourselves and our families from each is laid out in the word of God.

- Our defense from the world is to live lives separate from it. That involves not allowing it to enter our homes. We need to be wary of what of the world comes into our homes through the cable, the television, the radio, and the internet. As my wife and I were home schooling our children, we realized that the TV had to go. We eventually brought in a VCR and allowed them to watch carefully selected movies on Friday evenings but other than that, there was no TV.

- Our defense against the flesh is to recognize that, as believers, our old man is crucified with Christ and we do not need to let him run our lives anymore. We covered this in Chapter 4.

- Our defense against the devil is to recognize that he is a defeated enemy as far as his control of our lives is concerned. We must recognize that to embrace this freedom we must see ourselves in Christ and in the position that we have before God the Father in His Son.

It takes a stable marriage:

In America today, the number of kids growing up without a father being present in their lives is astounding. Among black Americans, 70% of kids grow up without a father who is married to the mother in the home. In 1965 that number was 25%. In the Hispanic community the number is about 50% and among whites it is over 25%. The single most visible reason for this situation is the social welfare system that rewards women by a system whereby they are incentivized to be (in effect) married to the state rather than to invest in the work required to maintain a stable marriage. Likewise, men can easily use this system to abdicate their responsibilities towards their children and the women who bore them.

At this point in our study we need the raise the question: "What does a stable marriage look like?" In the next chapter, we will study the institution of marriage along with the institution of the family. However, to answer that question simply here, I say that a stable marriage is the union of two spiritually mature saints (one man and one woman) joined to each other in the covenant of marriage. We will look at and answer the question "What constitutes spiritual maturity?" in Chapter 8 *Wisdom and Decision Making*. To answer the question of what a stable marriage looks like, I would direct people to 1Corinthians 13:4-7 where the apostle states what love is. The hallmark of spiritual maturity is the genuine unconditional love (Translated "Charity") that the apostle describes there. I quote the passage here:

> "⁴Charity suffereth long, *and* is kind; charity envieth not; charity vaunteth not itself, is not puffed up, ⁵Doth not behave itself unseemly, seeketh not her own, is not easily provoked, thinketh no evil; ⁶Rejoiceth not in iniquity, but rejoiceth in the truth; ⁷ Beareth all things, believeth all things, hopeth all things, endureth all things." (1 Corinthians 13:4-7)

Such love is the fruit that is naturally borne by the Spirit (Gal. 5:22-23) as a believer walks after the Spirit. We might also describe what an unstable marriage looks like. One can picture such a marriage by imagining union in which one or both parties are walking after the flesh. While the Spirit produces its sweet fruit of love, the flesh always produces its destructive works described in Galatians 5:19-21.

Teach your children at home: Whether you have your children in a public school, a private school or if you are home schooling them, the most important input into their education is what you can give them in the home. One of the key activities in the growth and maturity of children is their interaction with mature adults. The ultimate goal of maturing of children is that the children know how to think critically. We teach them this not by just telling them what the truth is but in instructing them as to why it is true. Maintaining an open channel of communication with your children is essential. They need to feel comfortable in talking with you about what is coming at them in their world. My wife and I found that the best format for that communication is in regular family devotions. These devotions would include a Bible reading, some prayer time and most importantly, free and open discussion of real life experiences and what the Bible has to say about them. It is especially important if your children are in public schools. It is in the open and free dialogue that they can feel free to bring up what they are hearing and to then go to the Word of God to seek divine wisdom on the matter at hand.

Family Devotions:

In our home, as the children were growing up, we would devotions with the children just before bed time. That was the time that they seemed to be wound up the most so it took s bit to quite them down to setting into the routine. We would do that by opening up with prayer. Then we would pick a passage of scripture and go around the room starting with the oldest and on around to the youngest. The youngest, who would be sitting next to mom, was likely just learning to read. She would read a word or two; often just sounding out the word. What amazed me though is how the questions would come out at that time. It would amaze me at how much thinking had be going on in their heads that did not or would not have come out had it not been for this opportunity afforded to them by the devotions and the Bible reading. We would limit the time to 15 minutes to half and hour so has not to make it seem to them as a chore. The devotions would then close with a round of prayer; again starting with the eldest and down to the youngest. This was an important learning experience for them is learning how to pray and to do so publically. These devotions should be headed up by dad it he is available. This is a key point in family life for dad to have a presence for the spiritual direction of the home.

On the Matter of Home Schooling:

My wife and I had the joy of raising five precious daughters. I thank the Lord that we were able to home school all five. This was not an easy task but it was truly a fruitful endeavor with blessed results. All five went on to further education to obtain college degrees with honors. Not that it is necessary that children go on the get an advanced degree but that each child can be equipped with the intellectual wherewithall to live a fruitful and godly life. The thought of home schooling your own children is daunting as you consider the sacrifice (including the fact that you will likely be living off of a single income) that you make in having to stay at home and the investment in time and funds in planning a school curriculum for each of your children year by year. However, there are home school associations in essentially every larger community in America. There are many excellent home school curriculums out there that can be tailor made to fit any child's learning style. I doubt that there is any state where there is not an annual home school convention where the vendors of the various curriculums are put on display.

CHAPTER 6
THE INSTITUTIONS OF GOD FOR
A FUNCTIONAL SOCIETY

We saw in Chapter 2 that God created man for an eternal purpose. He states that purpose in Hebrews 2:5-8 and there we see also how that purpose centers on Christ. "⁵ For unto the angels hath he not put in subjection the world to come, whereof we speak. ⁶ But one in a certain place testified, saying, What is man, that thou art mindful of him? or the son of man, that thou visitest him? ⁷ Thou madest him a little lower than the angels; thou crownedst him with glory and honour, and didst set him over the works of thy hands: ⁸ Thou hast put all things in subjection under his feet. For in that he put all in subjection under him, he left nothing *that is* not put under him. But now we see not yet all things put under him. ⁹ But we see Jesus, who was made a little lower than the angels for the suffering of death, crowned with glory and honour; that he by the grace of God should taste death for every man."

In order for man to be able to function orderly in society, God instituted divine operating principle that we call institutions. We call them Divine Institutions because God is the originator of them. Let's take a brief look at each of them.

Societal Institutions

Volition: The first of these institutions is volition. God created man as a free moral agent. An agent is someone who acts. A free agent is one who acts without external constraint. A free moral agent is one who acts without constraints on him but acts based on an internal system of moral ethics and standards. He is free in that he is free to make decisions in life and then acts on those decisions. God respects those decisions but will ultimately hold man responsible for what decisions he makes. Man is moral in that he has to capacity to know right from wrong. Man is an individual agent in that God sets him free to act independently but again He holds man accountable for the actions that he takes. We see the institution of volition in its primal form in Genesis 2:16 -17 in the instruction that God give to this newly formed creature – man. "¹⁶ And the LORD God commanded the man, saying, Of every tree of the garden thou mayest freely eat: ¹⁷ But of the tree of the knowledge of good and evil, thou shalt not eat of it: for in the day that thou eatest thereof thou shalt surely die." Man, at his creation, was totally free to do what he would with but one limitation – not to eat of the fruit of one particular tree.

There are four races of free moral agents created by God. There are angels, cherubim, seraphim, and us the members of this human race. We are quite different from the first three listed here. They live in the spirit world but we live in a three dimensional world of the space-matter-time continuum of earth. In their world, they see God and talk to God face to face. We, however, learn about God in a book (the Bible). We can not see God but we know about Him from what He has revealed to us in His Word. As we make decisions that please God based on information in the Word of God, we become a great witness to the principalities and powers in the spirit world (Eph. 3:10).

Marriage: We see the institution of marriage in Genesis 2: 21 -25 "21 And the LORD God caused a deep sleep to fall upon Adam, and he slept: and he took one of his ribs, and closed up the flesh instead thereof; 22 And the rib, which the LORD God had taken from man, made he a woman, and brought her unto the man. 23 And Adam said, This *is* now bone of my bones, and flesh of my flesh: she shall be called Woman, because she was taken out of Man. 24 Therefore shall a man leave his father and his mother, and shall cleave unto his wife: and they shall be one flesh." Man was created as a free moral agent who could reproduce more free moral agents and to do so indefinitely. It is in the institution of marriage that the propagation of the human race was to be accomplished.

One of the saddest commentaries on modern society is how the institution of marriage has been undermined and profaned. The result is that society at large has been rendered highly dysfunctional. The most important functional element of society is the institution of marriage with the family following as a close second in importance. The majority of social problems that society deals with today could be eliminated if man would follow the God ordained order for sexual expression – that being that one does not engage in sexual intercourse until he is married, does not get married until he is ready to be married, and once married he indeed is married and stays married for life.

In God's plan for man regarding sexuality sexual intimacy is reserved for marriage (Matt. 19:5 & 6; Eph. 5:31) and is to be freely enjoyed in the context of marriage (Hebrews 13:4). It is not for use outside of marriage (1Cor. 6:19). The concept of the husband and wife (male and female) being one flesh describes the intimacy that is part of the marriage contract. It is a great travesty on the institution of marriage for people to simply start living together without being married. The Lord's view on marriage is seen by His statement to the woman at the well in John 4:18 "... Thou hast had five husbands and he whom thou now hast is not thy husband..." Clearly, just living together did not constitute marriage that the Lord recognized. Marriage begins with a public ceremony with a public exchange of vows expressing a pledge of fidelity that lasts as long as both live (Rom. 7:3; 1Cor. 7:39). Our Lord further honored the institution by performing His first public miracle at a wedding (John 2:1-11).

"So God created man in his *own* image, in the image of God created he him; male and female created he them." (Genesis 1:26-27) God then makes an observation (actually it was more of a statement of fact) "18 And the LORD God said, It *is* not good that the man should be alone; I will make him an help meet for him. (Genesis 2:18) "21 And the LORD God caused a deep sleep to fall upon Adam, and he slept: and he took one of his ribs, and closed up the flesh instead thereof; 22 And the rib, which the LORD God had taken from man, made he a woman, and brought her unto the man. 23 And Adam said, This *is* now bone of my bones, and flesh of my flesh: she shall be called Woman, because she was taken out of Man. 24 Therefore shall a man leave his father and his mother, and shall cleave unto his wife: and they shall be one flesh." (Genesis 2:21-24)

"And they two shall be one flesh..." is the institution of marriage. It is the intimate union of a man and a woman (male and female) whereby they function together as one unit that becomes the type of the union of Christ and the church the Body of Christ (Eph. 4:32). Marriage is:

- Instituted as a special covenant of companionship.

- A special intimacy that exists no where else in the human race.

- A physical intimacy that parallels the spiritual intimacy of Christ and the Church. (Matt. 19:5 &6; 1Cor. 6:16; Eph. 5:31 &32). See also John 4:17 &18.

- This institution of marriage has a dispensational aspect to it. This aspect is addressed in Appendix 4 "Marriage, Divorce, and Remarriage in the Dispensation of Grace."

Family: The natural result of marriage is then the family. God's injunction to man to be fruitful and multiply and to replenish the earth is simply to have children whom they would then bring up in the nurture and admonition of the Lord. Married couples have children who then in turn have children with the result of the formation of society. The family is the main building block of society and of all effective social order. (Eph. 6:4; Psalm 127:3 &4) The commission that God gave to Adam and Eve: "28 Be fruitful and multiply and replenish the earth..." (Genesis 1:28) is the institution of family. There is an important consideration in regard to the family in God's plan for his creation. There are actually four different races of free moral agents that we encounter in the Bible. There are Cherubim, Seraphim, Angels and, of course, the human race. The first three of these exist in the spirit world where they can see God and speak directly to Him. We made reference to this in Chapter 1 when we talked about children's need for a structured social life.

As we study these races of free moral agents in the Word of God, we find that only one is designed by the creator to be able to reproduce itself – that being the human race. There is a stark difference between the human race and those races in the spirit world. Our knowledge of God in this human race is limited to what we read of Him in a book (the Bible). Our interaction with God is also limited. We can carry on a two way conversation with God but it is indirect. He speaks to us through His written word and we speak to Him in prayer. That then leads to the need for a social order for the protection of the family. That brings us to the next divine institution – that of nationalism. Nationalism becomes the means of social order to provide civil government in which family life can safely exist in a world that would be hostile toward innocent children. Family life therefore becomes very important in the propagation of godly generations. We saw the importance of family life in Chapter 5 in the section "A Lesson from the Rechabites."

The traditional family of a husband (a father and provider), a wife, (a mother and caregiver) and children under their care has been the underpinning of every great civilization in world history. It is a sad commentary that such an institution can be so much under attack as we see it in modern day America. Also alarming is the fact that in America (and in many western countries) human society in not reproducing itself. Statically, it takes about 2.1 children (average) per woman in order for a society to reach replacement level. In America, that replacement rate is at less than 1.5 children per woman. Were it not for immigration, we would not be replacing ourselves.

There is an active campaign going on in this world and especially here in America that militates against the family. The apparent goal of this campaign is to suppress the human race from reproducing itself according to the God given commission to "be fruitful and multiply and replenish the earth." (Gen. 1:27) We see it in the New World Order and particularly as it is expressed in the World Economic Forum (WEF) that suggests that the world is over populated and is beyond the carrying capacity by a factor of 10. Considering that the commission of Genesis 1:28 has never been rescinded, we are compelled to conclude that this goal is a satanically inspired ploy to foil God's plan for man.

Satan's arsenal of weapons in this campaign against children includes: the LGPTQ movement, the abortion industry, the same sex marriage nonsense, the tarn-sexual movement that envisions that a person can change their gender leaving them incapable of having children, and we can add to that list the double income - no kids mindset that seems to prevail in the college educated professional class of the 21ˢᵗ century. These trends all have their roots in the atheistic mindset that has been trending since the mid 1990's. That atheism has taken over the education institutions at all levels, the media, the entertainment industry, and also largely it seems in the corporate board rooms as well. That atheism has now morphed into a paganism that attributes time and chance as the creator of the universe and has man as the gods of the new age.

Nationalism: We see the institution of nationalism in Genesis 11:6-8 after the confusion of tongues at Babel. Satan had attempted to block God's plan to redeem man by the seed of the woman in Genesis 3:15 by corrupting the seed line. The flood of Noah's day was God's counter to that effort. He then sought to unite humanity against God at Babel. The effect of Babel would have been an unholy union of Satan and man which sought to prevent God from enjoying His creation and His fellowship with man by the creation of a one world government that would exclude God from that fellowship with man. God countered that one world government mentality by the confusion of tongues and the creation of a separation that would require nations to provide for the orderly function of society. "⁶And the LORD said, Behold, the people *is* one, and they have all one language; and this they begin to do: and now nothing will be restrained from them, which they have imagined to do. ⁷ Go to, let us go down, and there confound their language, that they may not understand one another›s speech. ⁸ So the LORD scattered them abroad from thence upon the face of all the earth: and they left off to build the city." (Genesis 11:6-8) This is God's work of intervention to stop the action by man that we would regard as globalism today. Genesis Chapter 11 documents a threefold giving up of man by God as is defined for us in Romans 1:24-28

> "²⁴ Wherefore God also gave them up to uncleanness through the lusts of their own hearts, to dishonour their own bodies between themselves: ²⁵ Who changed the truth of God into a lie, and worshipped and served the creature more than the Creator, who is blessed for ever. Amen. ²⁶ For this cause God gave them up unto vile affections: for even their women did change the natural use into that which is against nature: ²⁷ And likewise also the men, leaving the natural use of the woman, burned in their lust one toward another; men with men working that which is unseemly, and receiving in themselves that recompence of their error which was meet. ²⁸ And even as they did not like to retain God in *their* knowledge, God gave them over to a reprobate mind, to do those things which are not convenient;..."

The establishment of sovereign nations served God's interests in several ways. First, the existence of sovereign free nations gives to people on earth the opportunity to flee from oppressive governments in one county to another where there is freedom. Secondly, it stopped the action of man to create a one world government that sought to exclude God and deny Him the privilege of enjoying His creation. One day there will be a one world government that is ordained of God. That is what the Bible calls "the Kingdom of Heaven" in which God's will is going to be done in earth as it is in heaven. Until then, God's established order is for men to be subject to the powers that be as we read in Romans 13:1-6

"¹ Let every soul be subject unto the higher powers. For there is no power but of God: the powers that be are ordained of God. ² Whosoever therefore resisteth the power, resisteth the ordinance of God: and they that resist shall receive to themselves damnation. ³ For rulers are not a terror to good works, but to the evil. Wilt thou then not be afraid of the power? do that which is good, and thou shalt have praise of the same: ⁴ For he is the minister of God to thee for good. But if thou do that which is evil, be afraid; for he beareth not the sword in vain: for he is the minister of God, a revenger to *execute* wrath upon him that doeth evil. ⁵ Wherefore *ye* must needs be subject, not only for wrath, but also for conscience sake. ⁶ For for this cause pay ye tribute also: for they are God›s ministers, attending continually upon this very thing."

Globalism and Secularism verses Bible Believing Christianity

America has been blessed such that it has emerged as hegemony in this world since the 1940's. Conservative thought wants to Make America Great Again (the MAGA movement). However, we must first ask and answer the question: "What could made America great in the first place?" Those people who make an honest search as to what was the underpinnings that enabled this country to occupy that role, must conclude that it was Bible Believing Christianity which produced the traditional Christian home. Therefore, those that seek to dislodge America from that hegemonic position understand that their first task is to destroy the home and the family.

Redemptive Institutions

These first four institutions are what could be called societal institutions. They provide for the orderly functioning of society. There are yet other institutions that we could call redemptive institutions.

Atonement: There is yet another institution that we find in Genesis though it is not as well or as clearly defined in the Genesis account as the others are. That is the institution of the blood atonement. We see it with the clothing that God provided to Adam and Eve in Genesis 3:21 "²¹ Unto Adam also and to his wife did the LORD God make coats of skins, and clothed them." The first blood shed in creation was shed by innocent animals which were sacrificed to cover man's nakedness. Man knew that he was naked as soon as sin entered his consciousness. That sense of nakedness was due to the loss of innocence. From that point on in history, we can see in the record of scripture that every person regarded as a just man could identify a blood sacrifice that covered that lack of innocence. Adam at his creation was to have dominion over the fish of the sea, the foul of the air, over all cattle and over all of the earth. When he sinned he lost that dominion. When our Lord Jesus Christ came, He demonstrated dominion over the elements of the earth (Mark 4:33) and even over the spirit world (Mark 5:9-11). The only way for man to ever be what he was created to be is to find it in the atoning, redeeming work of Jesus Christ. From Genesis Chapter Three on in the Bible, every just or justified man could identify a blood sacrifice by which he could find the forgiveness of sins.

In summary then, the institutions of God include societal institutions of: Volition, Marriage, Family, and Nationalism. These institutions enable human society to function effectively in the world today. There is also the redemptive institution of the blood atonement for the remission of sins. We find it first with the coats of animal skins that the Lord provided to Adam and Eve to cover their nakedness after they sinned in Eden. From Genesis Chapter 3 (with the entrance of sin into the human history) there has always been a blood sacrifice whereby people can find atonement for their sin. We see it in Chapter Three as a covering for Adam's and Eve's sin. We see it in Chapter Four in God's plea to Cain to take advantage of that provision of that same sacrificial atonement which Abel made. We can trace it through the Bible until we find it in Romans 3:21-26 where it is clearly defined as "...the redemption that is in Christ Jesus: Whom God hath set forth *to be* a propitiation through faith in his blood..."

> "24 Being justified freely by his grace through the redemption that is in Christ Jesus: 25 Whom God hath set forth *to be* a propitiation through faith in his blood, to declare his righteousness for the remission of sins that are past, through the forbearance of God; 26 To declare, *I say*, at this time his righteousness: that he might be just, and the justifier of him which believeth in Jesus..." (Romans 3:24-26)

Marriage: God creates man in His own image in Adam. He then took a rib out of Adam and made a woman, brought her unto Adam and they two as husband and wife became one flesh. Thus we have the institution of marriage as male and female joined as one flesh.

Family: Adam and Eve as husband and wife become the progenitors of the human race with the propensity to reproduce more of the free moral agents that we know as the human race. Family life therefore becomes very important in the propagation of godly generations and the successful propagation of the human race. We saw the importance of family life in Chapter 5 in the section "A Lesson from the Rechabites."

The traditional family of a husband (a father and provider), a wife, (a mother and caregiver) and children under their care has been the underpinning of every great civilization in world history. It is a sad commentary that such an institution can be so much under attack as we see it in modern day America. Also alarming is the fact that in America (and in many western countries) human society in not reproducing itself. Statically, it takes about 2.1 children (average) per woman in order for a society to reach replacement level. In America, that replacement rate is at less than 1.5.

Nationalism: Nationalism is an institution of God but it was instituted to counter the globalism that man devised in Genesis 11: 1-6. We see the nationalism in Genesis 11:7 &8. Nationalism is the concept of sovereign nations with a border, a culture, and a language.

Redemptive Institutions

There are also things instituted by God for the purpose of Redemption.

Atonement: This is first evidenced in Genesis by the blood sacrifice of the animal that shed its blood to cover Adam and Eve's nakedness. This shed blood represented the surrender of innocent life – the sacrifice that provided the skins that replaced the fig leaves of Genesis 3.

Eternal life might be considered an institution of God but God had eternal life in view from the time man was created. It is just that death entered into man's life as a temporary interruption of that life. All redeemed people have eternal life. Such redemption was in God's plan from before man was created. (Romans 6:23; Titus 1:1 &2)

CHAPTER 7
DISCIPLINE, DISCIPLES AND DISCIPLESHIP -

Children are amazing little creatures. They are each born into a family as an awesome testimony to the creative genius and power of our creator. They are a witness to the wise design of the creator who created a race of free moral agents who can reproduce more such free moral agents. As amazing as they are, they do not come into our families as finished products. They enter our homes as precious little bundles of potentiality. Children are each unique individuals who are a part of the creator's eternal purpose for man. However, their hope of learning about that eternal purpose is rests in us their parents. There is much teaching, molding, and shaping to be done. The ultimate finished product is a mature saint in the kingdom of God. That finishing involves the science and art of discipline (including the self discipline that they employ themselves as they mature) and discipleship from parents and teachers. Let's talk about that in this chapter.

Discipline, Disciples, and Discipleship

What we do mean by discipline? As a noun, a "discipline" speaks of a branch of knowledge that requires a certain amount of expertise. We can talk about academic and scientific disciplines such as engineering, medicine, law, etc. These disciplines prepare the professional for the occupation by which they earn a living in this world. These are academic disciplines that hone one's skills relative to a chosen profession as apposed to the generalist. However, the discipline that we talk about with regard to parenting focuses on the developing of life skills – the skills that will ultimately make the child equipped for success as a fully functional adult. These are the life skills that everyone needs to function well in society.

Some Definition o f Terms:

Discipline

A general discipline of life is necessary to live a happy and fulfilling life. Such a discipline includes life skills such as keeping personal spaces in order, maintaining personal hygiene, keeping physically fit and healthy, especially by maintaining a healthy diet (a challenge given the current American carbohydrate and sugar rich diet). Included in such a discipline of life today would be making judicial use of social media to avoid its addictive influence, learning how to balance a budget, and making wise use of that precious resource called "time."

Chastisement:

> To inflict corporal punishment with the view to adjust behavior patterns. Chastisement is withdrawn when the child submits to loving parental authority.

Punishment:

> Punishment is the administering of justice for the breaking of an established standard. For justice and consistency's sake, punishment must be enforced whenever is due. This applies whether or not repentance and submission is made.

Self Discipline:

> This is the discipline of self. Introspection is an important quality in both parents and in children as they mature and move into taking charge of their own discipline. Self discipline involves introspection that is based on what the Bible sets forth as the qualities that we look for in ourselves and in our children. A good place to start as to what should be in our lives is Philippians 4:8-9. For a list of things that should be purged from our lives one would be well advised to start with the list in 2Timothy 3:2-8 on traits of men in the last days of the dispensation of grace.

Discipline can basically be thought of as the making of a disciple. In simple terms, a disciple is a kind of a student who follows the teaching of, learns from, and models his life after another (i.e. after a mentor). In the Christian home, the teacher (the mentor) is the parent and the student is the child. The term "discipleship" is also pertinent to the process. Instilling discipline is the process of making disciples of our children that they might ultimately function as mature adults.

My wife would often use the term "shaping and molding" with regard to the process of what we call here discipleship. There are actually three elements to discipleship: First, there is the teaching element. What we teach as Christian parents is the Word of God. This is what we would call teaching Bible Doctrine. This involves studying the Word of God to the end result that neither we nor our children need ever be ashamed of our understanding of the doctrine. We do that by "rightly dividing the Word of truth" (2Timothy 2:15). Secondly, there is a learning process that involves acquiring of the life skills that prepares the child to be successfully self-sufficient in adulthood. This involves being healthy and well adjusted in our entire makeup of spirit, soul, and body (1Thessalonians 5:23). Thirdly, there is a modeling aspect to parenting. It is not just what you say (or demand) as a parent that produces the adult but, probably more importantly, it is what you model. Simply put, it takes a disciple to produce a disciple. Honesty, diligence, faithfulness, and courage are examples of virtues that are acquired by seeing them admired and appreciated when we see them and observe them in our mentor – our parents in the case of parenting.

As Christian parents, we are concerned about our children being not only fully equipped for personal life but to also function as a member of the church the body of Christ. That being the case, we would probably best define the activity of discipleship by a Bible verse that clearly lays out the roles of both the mentor and the student. After all, as we noted, a disciple is actually a student who has a mentor. A disciple follows the teaching of his mentor; he learns from him and models his life after what he sees in his mentor. As we think about parenting, discipleship certainly does relate to the parent-child relationship. There is a verse in 2 Timothy that defines the role of both the mentor and the student very well. I present it here for consideration.

> "[1] Thou therefore, my son, be strong in the grace that is in Christ Jesus. [2] And the things that thou hast heard of me among many witnesses, the same commit thou to faithful men, who shall be able to teach others also." (2 Timothy 2:1-2)

As we consider this passage written by Paul to the young man Timothy, we understand first of all that Timothy was to be strong in the grace that is in Christ Jesus himself. What Paul is telling Timothy is what we stated above -- that it takes a disciple to produce a disciple. What Timothy learned from Paul he was to pass on to others who would in turn pass on to still others. This speaks of the generational propagation of what should be the normal Christian life. We note first that Paul modeled the Christian life for Timothy. Paul is urging him to model that for the benefit of other men who would in turn model it to still others.

There is a certain learning process in discipleship. The apostle speaks of this learning process in Philippians 4: 8-9 saying "[8] Finally, brethren, whatsoever things are true, whatsoever things *are* honest, whatsoever things *are* just, whatsoever things *are* pure, whatsoever things *are* lovely, whatsoever things *are* of good report; if *there be* any virtue, and if *there be* any praise, think on these things. [9] Those things, which ye have both learned, and received, and heard, and seen in me, do: and the God of peace shall be with you." Here we see Paul telling the Philippians what the Christian life should look like. They learned it not only by what Paul said to them but also by what Paul modeled in his life among them.

Progressive Discipline and Discipleship

Discipline and discipleship needs to be progressive. It needs to advance progressively according to the stage of development of each child. In Chapter 3 we considered how the natural growth and development of a child goes through stages from total dependence through independence to fully functional interdependence. Our parenting style changes as the child grows and develops through these stages. The child going through the "terrible twos" will require a different approach to discipline than the preteen or teen. Discipline done properly up to about age ten will (we trust) bring the peaceable fruits of righteousness (see Hebrews 12:11) in the teen. In adulthood, children (as do we the parents) move into the interdependence of those who function in social order such as family, business, and fellowship. This is where discipline becomes self discipline. Here, the disciple becomes his own mentor. In self discipline, one makes a disciple of oneself. One is then one's own teacher, trainer, coach, and disciplinarian. It is an odd sort of a relationship. Unfortunately, not everyone handles it well. There is much unhappiness and distress in the world because of our personal failures to control our tempers, appetites, passions, and urges. True freedom comes only to one who has mastered the control of self.

As Christians, we approach discipline differently than does the typical secular world. That is because we as Bible believers see people (human nature) differently than does the secular world. The world in general (what we might call secularism) sees all people as being basically good. Secularism would blame outside influences for bad behavior. The United Nations, for example, had a convention of the Right of the Child (see on the UN web site the Convention of the Right of the Child) in which they conclude that basically any form of corporal punishment is inappropriate. Bible believing Christianity, however, sees a malfunctioning conscience as the cause of bad behavior. We understand that our children were born with the same sin nature that we, their parents, were born with. We therefore understand that our objective is to adjust the conscience so that children learn that right and wrong is not based on how we feel about it but on what the Word of God has to say about it. We have what should be a final authority for our decisions but that final authority is not our feelings. It is as Jeremiah says about our feelings: "[9] The heart *is* deceitful above all *things*, and desperately wicked: who can know it? [10] I the LORD search the heart, *I* try the reins, even to give every man according to his ways, *and* according to the fruit of his doings."(Jeremiah 17:9-10)

Speaking of conscience, we are talking about the knowledge of right and wrong with respect to what we hold as truth. It is the system by which we make decisions and take actions in life. The Bible says a lot about the conscience. A conscience can be good and pure (Acts 23:1; 24:16; 1Tim. 1:5, 19; 3:19; 2Tim. 1:3; etc.). A conscience can also be weak and defiled (Titus 1:5; 1Tim. 4:2; etc.)

The world says that truth is subjective – depending on one's personal opinion. If truth were subjective, then there would be no absolute standard of right and wrong. We as Bible believers however, say truth is objective and that there is such a thing as absolute truth. That final authority is available to man in the Word of God – the Bible. To submit to objective truth and the objective morality of the Word of God, is to have an absolute standard of right and wrong that is outside of us. It is therefore important that children (and parents) understand that ultimately we will each give an account to our Lord Jesus Christ as to what we did with the truth of the Word of God and with the eternal life that we, as believers, received as a gift of God's grace.

What we are providing for our children is a Bible based moral compass. We therefore understand that there is a need for a prudent application of what the Bible calls "the rod." The Bible reference to the rod is referring to corporal punishment – physical punishment that result in some pain and discomfort to the child. Such punishment should be kept to the very minimum that is needed to address misbehavior. Being negative in nature, corporal punishment is stressful to the child and usually more so to the parent who finds himself or herself having to administer it. When we speak of corporal punishment, we are referring to what is commonly called a spanking. It is typically applicable for children between the ages of two and ten. Corporal punishment must never injure a child in any way. A swat on the buttocks will not injure a child but it will communicate that mom and/or dad do mean business. It must be always administered in loving concern for the child.

Christian parents need to bear in mind that Bible based discipline can include (when the situation warrants it) some chastisement of a corporal nature. Here is where great love, patience and wisdom are needed. Paul gives special instructions to fathers with regard to parenting saying in Ephesians 6:4 "And, ye fathers, provoke not your children to wrath: but bring them up in the nurture and admonition of the Lord."

It should be noted that the secular world's view on chastening is different than is the Bible based view. Scripture sees chastening as an expression of love for our children. There are some notable Old Testament passages that are instructive on the subject. They are presented here for your consideration:

Proverbs 13:24 "He that spareth his rod hateth his son: but he that loveth him chasteneth him betimes." Bear in mind that he Bible word "hate" does not carry the same meaning as does our modern usage. The thought here is that a parent who refuses to chasten his child does not have the love for him that one with deep concern for the child's well being should have.

Proverbs 19:18 "Chasten thy son while there is hope, and let not thy soul spare for his crying." Time is of the essence in childrearing. Loving discipline rendered from early childhood on through adolescent and teen years administered when needed is sure to succeed while neglecting to chasten misses a key window of opportunity.

Proverbs 22:15 "Foolishness *is* bound in the heart of a child; *but* the rod of correction shall drive it far from him." Children need help to get control over their emotions. Every child is an amazing work of divine creation. However, in each is a little monster that seeks to express itself. All it takes is laxity on the part of mom and dad to release him.

Parental Authority and Posture

Parental authority must be maintained from infancy on with children. There is what we call posture. Posture expresses itself in the unspoken understanding that communicates simple principles of practice with children. Posture communicates to children is when mom and dad tell the child to do something, for the child to not do it is not an option. Likewise, when mom and dad tell the child to do some certain thing, for the child to not do it is likewise not an option. Consistency from infancy on is the key to maintaining such posture.

Understanding Obedience:

Discipline is a progressive exercise between parent and child. It is necessary that the parent impress upon their children the need for obedience as a part of their loving concern for the welfare of their children. Properly done, the children will pick up on the exercise and take responsibility to carry their part in the program. The parents have a responsibility to require obedience. Otherwise there is no purpose in instructing children to obey. Parents must, from infancy on, impress upon their children the need to listen, understand, and follow parental instruction. The discipline of children is a parental role and a parental responsibility. One thing that ought to be obvious here is that this role and responsibility cannot be carried out by absentee parents. Children can not learn to obey parents who are not there.

Ephesians 6:1-4
[1] Children, obey your parents in the Lord: for this is right. [2] Honour thy father and mother; (which is the first commandment with promise;) [3] That it may be well with thee, and thou mayest live long on the earth. [4] And, ye fathers, provoke not your children to wrath: but bring them up in the nurture and admonition of the Lord. (Eph. 6:1-4)

The word "obey" is from a compound word meaning literally "to hear under." The concept is: 1) to hear, 2) to understand and 3) to act according to those instructions. This is the same verb used in Romans 6:17 on obedience to the gospel and in Ephesians 6:5 on obedience of servants to masters.

Understanding Disobedience

Disobedience can be understood as existing on three different levels. They are: Non accountable disobedience, Accountable disobedience, and Rebellious disobedience. The difference between these is in relation to how the proper standard of conduct was understood. Let's consider each and consider how each should be addressed.

Non Accountable Disobedience:

Occurs for a variety of reasons:

- The child did not know the standard.

- The standard was not accurately communicated.

- No standard has been previously established for that offense.

- The standard was not consciously broken.

In such cases the child should not be held accountable and no penalty should be enforced (Romans 4:15b; 5:13b) A rebuke, however, is needed to establish the standard. The rebuke needs to be strong enough that the standard is internalized.

Accountable Disobedience

The standard is established, it has been communicated, and it was internalized. If asked, the child can verbalize the standard. The child should be held accountable and the penalty must be paid. (Romans 4:15a; 6:13a; Genesis 2:17) The child admits to the violation and does not act in rebellion to the authority.

Rebellious Disobedience

In this case, the standard is fully known. The child, knowing the standard and the consequences of violating the standard, operates in rebellion to both the standard and the authority. This is disrespect for and rebellion against both the standard and the authority (i.e. the parents) that established it (1 Timothy 2:14; Genesis 3:1-7; 1 Samuel 1:8-14). Left to fully develop its full potential, this heart attitude would be the making of a criminal mind.

The child has set his will against the will of the parents and has entered into a contest of wills. When, in the parent-child relationship, a contest of wills arises, the will of the loving parents (having the eternal and the temporal welfare of the child in mind) must prevail. This is a test of parental love, persistence of purpose, prayerful patience, and wisdom. Here is where the political capital of a lifetime of demonstrated loving concern for the child pays off. Here is where mom and dad draw upon consistency with the child through the years to win the emotional conflict, gain a spiritual victory, and save a precious relationship.

Handling Disobedience, Defiance, and Rebellion

Normally, children who are usually under authority but occasionally disobey do so an act of childishness. Such children will admit to their wrong when rebuked. They should be forgiven and the appropriate punishment administered without corporal punishment.

Rebellious children are those who do not admit to their rebellious attitude when rebuked. However, they can be brought to the point of confession by the use of reasonable corporal punishment. They will admit to their guilt, confess their wrong, and seek to be restored to fellowship with the parents. This type of rebellion is generally found in strong willed children between the ages of 3 and 12.

Hardened children are those who are in rebellion and will not (even under consistent chastisement) acknowledge their guilt or rebellion. Properly handling rebellion in the child will require a great deal of prayer and a clear manifestation of parental love for and to the child. Often the parents must first, after serious soul searching, acknowledge (first to himself and then to the child) any misapplication of discipline in the past (Eph. 6:4). Here is where much prayer and wisdom on the parent's part is essential. In such a situation, the child must be chastened consistently to bring them under the authority of the parents but such chastening must be done with love and respect for the child's person. Here is where the parent draws upon the equity gained from past investments of parental love in the child's life pays dividends. Just as "the fear of the LORD is the beginning of wisdom (Job 28:28; Psalm 111:10), so too, a rebellious child begins to have wisdom when he responds to parental authority so as to respect it. This type of rebellion typically applies to youths 12 years old and older, who have not been under authority while younger or the child sees an injustice in the parent's treatment of him or her. These are what are called the strong willed children. These are the kids that eventually grow up to be the leaders of society but not until they mature enough to learn that authority is there for their own security and protection and for the purpose of order in society.

Chastisement of disobedient children must be:

1. Absolutely always administered in love.

2. Always with the acceptance and respect of the child as a person.

3. Always with consistent application at every occurrence of rebellion.

4. Absolutely always with much prayer and loving concern for the future welfare of the child.

Chastisement should be reserved for:

Open defiance of parental authority.

Action endangering another child

Willful destruction of property

And finally, Temper tantrums.

Understand that no child is happy while he or she is in rebellion. The child caused the problem by his rebellion and he needs his parent's help in conquering it. Note what is happening:

The child is miserable with himself.

His parents are unhappy with him.

He perceives himself as unacceptable to the family circle and thus feels separated.

The only way for the parents to demonstrate love is to chasten him to make his conduct acceptable to the family again.

Table 4 Extremes of Discipline

Too Harsh of discipline	Loving Discipline	No Discipline
Can produce a Self Deprecating attitude in the child.	Produces normal children well adjusted to life. The child sees himself / herself in Christ.	Can produce an egotistical Adult
The child struggles to accept self and may develop negative attitude towards others. The child might also struggle to find value and purpose in life	The child loves and accepts and respects self and others and has good balance in life	The child might or can tend to think more highly of himself than he ought to think

There are Two Extremes in Discipline that can produce undesired results, those being too harsh of discipline and (at the other extreme) no discipline.

Discipline and Self Esteem

Here is another area in which Bible based thinking differs from secularism. The world tends to hold the view that all men are basically good so it is good to let the natural man express itself. However, the Bible believer understands that the natural man receives not the things of the Spirit of God (1Cor. 2:14) and that the carnal mind is enmity against God and is not subject to the law of God (Rom. 8:7). The Bible believer understands that true self esteem comes from self control. Self control comes from obedience to a particular form of Bible doctrine (Rom. 6:17). A Bible verse that clearly brings that out is Romans 8:13-15. Note the apostle's instruction -- [13] For if ye live after the flesh, ye shall die: but if ye through the Spirit do mortify the deeds of the body, ye shall live. [14] For as many as are led by the

Spirit of God, they are the sons of God. [15] For ye have not received the spirit of bondage again to fear; but ye have received the Spirit of adoption, whereby we cry, Abba, Father. (Romans 8:13-15) To mortify is to "cause to die." The believer can not cause the sin nature to die but he can cause the outworking of the sin nature through the body to die. That is true self control and that is where true self esteem and true freedom comes from.

There is nothing wrong with loving oneself (Eph. 5:28). Love of oneself is necessary for: Self Preservation, Self Acceptance, Self Respect, and Self Confidence. Scripture presupposes that the well adjusted person will have a certain amount of love of himself.

- "Love your neighbor as yourself" (Lev. 19:18; Matt. 19:19; 22:39; et. al)

- "Love your wife as your own body" (Eph. 5:28)

But! It must be self respect without self centeredness, and self acceptance without pride and arrogance.

Examples of the wrong kind of discipline:

1. Unloving Chastening – Discipline that does not manifest a clear desire for both the eternal welfare of the child and his temporal welfare fails to equip him for life and for eternity. Loving discipline communicates to the child "I love you too much to let you get by with this bad conduct." Loving discipline is discipline motivated by concern for the child's total welfare and general well being (spiritually, emotionally, and physically). However, discipline that is motivated by the parent's selfish interests will likely engender wrath in the child (Eph. 6:4). If the parent's motivation says "I have my position in society so you have to conduct yourself accordingly to my position so I can maintain my image." This leads the child to ask himself "Are you interested in me and my needs and aspirations or is it your position that really concerns you?"

2. Chastening Administered in Anger – is not true discipline but is rather a contest for mastery. This is an example of conduct (anger) that we do not want to see duplicated in the child's character. No matter how angry or upset the parent might be, it is essential that he get control of the negative emotion so that it is only the love for the child that compels the parental response. Consider the following passages from Hebrews 12:6, 9, 10, and 11 on the subject of discipline:

> [5] And ye have forgotten the exhortation which speaketh unto you as unto children, My son, despise not thou the chastening of the Lord, nor faint when thou art rebuked of him: [6] For whom the Lord loveth he chasteneth, and scourgeth every son whom he receiveth. [7] If ye endure chastening, God dealeth with you as with sons; for what son is he whom the father chasteneth not? [8] But if ye be without chastisement, whereof all are partakers, then are ye bastards, and not sons. [9] Furthermore we have had fathers of our flesh which corrected *us*, and we gave *them* reverence: shall we not much rather be in subjection unto the Father of spirits, and live? [10] For they verily for a few days chastened *us* after their own pleasure; but he for *our* profit, that *we* might be partakers of his holiness. [11] Now no chastening for the present seemeth to be joyous, but grievous: nevertheless afterward it yieldeth the peaceable fruit of righteousness unto them which are exercised thereby. (Hebrews 12:5-11)

3. Unjust Discipline is bad discipline – We trust God to do right. Our children trust us to do right. Children have a well developed sense of right and wrong and therefore a good sense of justice. We need to know that the child knew the rule that was broken or the standard of conduct that was violated before chastening is administered. Children should never be disciplined for failing to do a task they were incapable of doing. Also, discipline must always be commensurate with the severity of the offence. We must be careful to mete out a penalty that is fair discipline according to the child's offence.

4. No Discipline is bad discipline -- Children need discipline. They need boundaries. Discipline means acceptance. No discipline is the act of ignoring the child's need for boundaries for their protection; it is indifference, laziness, and lack of concern. A lack of discipline actually communicates to the child that the parent is not interested in their conduct or their character. The worst thing you can do to a child is leave him to his own devices.

> [15] The rod and reproof give wisdom: but a child left *to himself* bringeth his mother to shame. [16] When the wicked are multiplied, transgression increaseth: but the righteous shall see their fall. [17] Correct thy son, and he shall give thee rest; yea, he shall give delight unto thy soul. Proverbs 29:15-17

5. Yelling is not discipline but is more in the area of verbal abuse. This is one of the areas where dad needs to step in when discipline is needed. There is a tendency when discipline is left to mom; it becomes more in the category of verbal threats. But when dad is called in, the discipline tends to go to a higher level. If a man does not take his God given position of being the head and ruler of the home, the "figure head" position of the home becomes blurred in the minds of the children. In the roles of moms and dads, a well run home has a high court of appeals in dad. A gentle, but firm mom operates in the home under the authority of a loving but firm dad.

Children need Boundaries.

This world is becoming an ever more dangerous place. We as parents therefore place boundaries (and fences) for our children to protect them from dangers that they might be oblivious to because of their innocent and trusting nature. They need to know that the boundaries are there for their protection from dangers. We need to think of boundaries as the safety shields that are placed on dangerous equipment for protection of the operator. Boundaries that are enforced by discipline are therefore essential in a world that is full of dangers for the child.

Boundaries that are well thought out, explained to the child, and properly enforced gives children a sense of safety and security. I am reminded of an account of a lady who was on a school board observing children at play in the fenced playground. She notice that the children were all playing out along the fence and even climbing on the fence. She concluded that the fence was stifling the children's creativity. Through her efforts on the school board, she succeeded in having the fence removed. Once the fence was removed, she then noticed that the children were not using the entire playground but were actually congregating in the center of the large area. What was happening was that the children, while the fence was in place, saw the fence as a safety net that separated from the dangerous world around them. While they were in the fenced boundary, they were safe to play and to utilize all of the freedom that was available to them by the large playground. So too, children who stay within well thought out and enforced boundaries, enjoy and utilize all of the freedom allotted to them. As children mature and demonstrate that they can handle more freedom, the boundaries are relaxed.

CHAPTER 8
WISDOM AND DECISION MAKING

Sons of God in Adulthood

Paul's epistles say a lot about wisdom. In fact they say a lot about knowledge, wisdom and understanding. Knowledge is simply a matter of knowing the facts on which to base decisions. Gaining knowledge is the quest for truth in how God works today in the Dispensation of Grace. Understanding goes a little further in that if explores what one holds to be true and knows why it is true. Wisdom is the ability to take that knowledge and and understanding and to then make the right decisions for the desired outcome based on the facts (the truth). If the desired outcome is godliness, then the knowledge involved is contained in and derived from the Word of God. Understanding then is the bedrock principle upon which knowledge and wisdom are founded.

Basing decisions on emotions is not wisdom. Our emotions are designed by God to follow our thinking. Once wise decisions are made based on the knowledge of the facts and God's revealed will, our emotions come into play to add energy to our decision. One of the critical skills that we develop in growing up to adulthood is how make wise decisions. We can learn much about how to make wise decisions from the Pauline epistles because he (Paul) is the revealer of God's will for us who live in the Dispensation of Grace. His epistles are therefore tailored by God to equip us to meet the life situations that we face in our world today.

We talked about how romance is involved in much of the exchange between the sexes – particularly during the latter teen years. I offer this excellent little excerpt from Dr. James Peterson taken from "Manual for Group Pre-marital Counseling" 1971 pp 56-57 Edited by Lyle B. Ganges

First, romance results in such distortions of personality that, after marriage the two people can never fulfill the roles that they expect of each other.

Second, romance so idealizes marriage and even sex that when the day to day experiences of marriage are encountered, there must be disillusionment involved.

Third, The romance complex is so short sighted that the pre-marriage relationship is conducted almost entirely on the emotional level and consequently such problems as temperament or value differences, religious or cultural differences, financial, occupational or health problems are never considered.

Fourth, romance develops such a false ecstasy that there is implied in courtship a promise of a kind of happiness which could never be maintained during the realities of married life.

Fifth, romance is such an escape from the negative aspects of personality to the extent that their repression obscures the real person. Later in marriage these negative factors to marital adjustment are bound to appear, and they were not evident earlier.

Sixth, people engrossed in romance seem to be prohibited from wise planning for the basic needs of the future even to the point of failing to discuss the significant problems of early marriage.

The way of wisdom -- an expose of 1Corinthians 1:1 to 2:7 and 13:1-13:

The Preaching of the Cross

"[18] For the preaching of the cross[a] is to them that perish[b] foolishness[c]; but unto us which are saved[d] it is the power of God. [19] For it is written, I will destroy the wisdom of the wise[e], and will bring to nothing the understanding of the prudent. [20] Where *is* the wise? where *is* the scribe? where *is* the disputer of this world? hath not God made foolish the wisdom of this world? [21] For after that in the wisdom of God the world by wisdom[f] knew not God, it pleased God by the foolishness of preaching to save[g] them that believe. [22] For the Jews require[h] a sign, and the Greeks seek after wisdom[i]: [23] But we preach Christ crucified, unto the Jews a stumblingblock, and unto the Greeks foolishness; [24] But unto them which are called[j], both Jews and Greeks, Christ the power of God, and the wisdom of God. [25] Because the foolishness of God is wiser than men[k]; and the weakness of God is stronger than men." (1Cor. 1:18-25)

[a] "The preaching of the cross" literally means the message of the cross. The cross itself is without significance, but what took place on it is the single-most significant event in the entire history of mankind. It was there that the eternal creator died on behalf of His creatures -- humanity (Rom. 5:6-8). The message of the cross is that man needs a Savior in order for individual members of it to be accepted into God's presence and into His kingdom.

[b] The words "To them that perish" in Verse 18 is in the present tense. That means that those who perish are in the in the process of ruin; they are in the process of dying. This is specifically referring to those who see no need for a Savior and therefore proceed on their way to eternal death without trusting Christ. The gospel that Christ died for our sins is "Foolishness" to those who view themselves as acceptable to God just as they are. The message or concept that God would have to enter humanity and to submit to execution as a criminal is a foolish and senseless notion (*cf* Gal 6:12) to such a person. The believer who faithfully proclaims Christ crucified (which he must do in order to see men saved) will therefore be mocked (Acts 17:18, 32) by those who do not see their lost condition.

[c] The words "...Unto us which are saved" is a verb form and is also in the present tense. It is referring to we (believers) who are in the process of being saved. Remember that there are three tenses to salvation:

1. The Past Tense -- Salvation from the penalty of sin (Acts 16:31; Rom. 3:25). This salvation made the believer secure.

2. The Present Tense -- Salvation from the power of sin (Rom 6:1-14; 1Cor. 15:2) makes the believer sanctified.

3. The Future Tense -- Salvation from the very presence of sin (Rom 13:17; 1Thess. 5:9) will make the believer glorified in the future with the catching away of the Body of Christ to heaven.

[d] Though the concept of a substitutionary atonement is foolishness to the one who sees no need for it, it is necessary to God and is, to the believer, the satisfaction of the righteous demands of God "…that he might be just, and the justifier of him which believes in Jesus" (Rom. 3:26).

[e] Paul here quotes Isaiah 29:14 where we see that the Lord will cause the wisdom of men (the wisdom that sees no need for the cross) to perish by doing "a marvelous work." We now know this marvelous work to be the "preaching of the cross." Paul asks three questions here and then answers them with yet a fourth question.

1. Where is the wise? (the intellectual)

2. Where is the scribe? (the expert in the law)

3. Where is the disputer of this world? (the debater)

There were none in the Corinthian assembly because:

- Neither the proclaiming of nor the receiving of salvation depends on human wisdom.

- Living under grace is independent of Law.

- There is no room for debate but there is room for the receiving of the simple but absolute truth.

The fourth question then is "Hath not God made foolish the wisdom of this world?" The answer to that question is Yes! (*cf* Job 12:17).

[f] Wisdom (real wisdom) belongs to God (Dan. 2:20). Here is a structural layout of 1Corinthians 1:21

> after that in the wisdom of God the world…..knew not God
> by wisdom [i.e. by the wisdom of God]

> For…..it pleased God…..to save them that believe"
> by the foolishness of preaching

God manifested His wisdom in creation (Rom 1:18-20). However, fallen man would not glorify Him as God but "became vain in their imaginations, and their foolish heart was darkened. Professing themselves to be wise, they <u>became fools</u>, and changed the glory of the incorruptible God into an image made like to corruptible man, and to birds, and four-footed beasts, and creeping things." (Rom 3:21-23). Such foolishness became the "wisdom of men". God cared too much for man to accept that kind of wisdom. Therefore, God displayed His wisdom in another way (i.e. preaching of the cross) and was pleased to save those who believe it. It was by the wisdom of God that "the world… knew not God…" for God:

"gave them up to uncleanness" (Rom. 1:24)

"gave them up to vile affections" (Rom. 1:26)

"gave them over to a reprobate mind" (Rom. 1:28)

It is now by the wisdom of God that the world can come to God by means of the cross.

[g] "To save" in Verse 22 is in the aorist tense and active voice. This is real action that God does on behalf of the believer the moment he or she believed. Here, as in Romans 3:22, we see the distinction between the unlimited provision of salvation and the limited application of it. It is provided for all (it is available to all) but is an actual possession of "them that believe."

[h] The Jews <u>require</u> a sign. The word "sign" here means a miraculous display of divine power. As a nation, they were conditioned by God to look for such signs and such were evident throughout our Lord's ministry to the nation (Matt. 10:6-8; Luke 2:34; John 4:48; Acts 2:22; 4:30). It was not inappropriate for Israel to <u>require</u> a sign, for that was a divinely provided safeguard from deception for the nation. When their Messiah came, they would recognize Him by certain signs (John 10:25-32).

[i] Paul says that the Greeks seek other wisdom -- this is the nature of the sophisticated unbeliever to this day. "But" in contrast to miraculous signs and worldly wisdom, we preach a crucified Messiah. Such a Messiah was to the Jews a stumbling block, for "...they...going about to establish their own righteousness, have not submitted themselves unto the righteousness of God" (Rom 10:3). Likewise, to the sophisticated Gentile, the notion that he needed a blood sacrifice was "foolishness" (*cf* Acts 17:19-20).

[j] "Them which are called" in Verse 24 is synonymous with "them that believe".

The order of events in salvation is:

1st the sinner hears the gospel,

2nd the sinner, recognizing that he, having a decision to make, believes the gospel.

3rd God does the work of regeneration and calls the believer to His Kingdom. This calling includes being predestinated (having a preset destiny) to glory. This destiny was set the moment one believed. God did not predestinate certain people to believe and, by default, predestinate others to not believe.

Romans 8:29 lays out this order of events in the believer's life as does Ephesians 1: 13 &14.

[k] What the unsaved world regards as foolishness (i.e. the cross) is in reality wiser than any wisdom that man has ever or will ever come up with. So too, the weakness of God manifested in the confessed weakness of the believer, is stronger than any strength that any man has.

[l] In Verse 24 Paul cites that there are not many wise among the brethren at Corinth. Though Paul is talking about all believers here, he is specifically drawing attention to those used of God to preach the gospel to the Corinthians. Not only in the "rank & file" but also in the leadership there were:

- Not many wise. Not that the gospel doesn't appeal to intelligent people, but that people who are enamored with human wisdom are not attracted to the gospel. The term "After the flesh" ia a reference to how the natural man views wisdom.

- Not many noble. Not many well born, or of a high social class.

God has chosen the Foolish things of the World

"26 For ye see your calling, brethren, how that not many wise[m] men after the flesh, not many mighty, not many noble, *are called*: 27 But God hath chosen[n] the foolish things of the world to confound the wise; and God hath chosen the weak things of the world to confound the things which are mighty; 28 And base things of the world, and things which are despised, hath God chosen, *yea*, and things which are not, to bring to nought things that are: 29 That no flesh should glory[n] in his presence. 30 But of him[o] are ye in Christ Jesus, who of God is made unto us wisdom, and righteousness, and sanctification, and redemption: 31 That, according as it is written[p], He that glorieth, let him glory in the Lord." (1Cor. 1:26-31)

[m] God has chosen: to:

- The foolish things of the world   confound the wise

- The weak things of the world   confound the things which are mighty

- The base things of the world   bring to naught things that are

- and things that are despised,   "

- and things which are not.   "

[n] Here, in Verse 27, the reason is given for God choosing the most unlikely candidates for glory: "That no flesh should glory in His presence". God will never be beholden to the flesh of man. So too, He will never share His glory with the flesh. All the glory will go to God (Matt. 6:13). God will leave no room for boasting on the part of prideful man (Eph. 2:9; 2Cor. 10:17).

[o] The words "Of him…" in Verse 30 literally means "out of Him". That is, out of God before whom no one might boast are we in Christ Jesus who "of God" (as an act of God) is made unto us:

- Wisdom -- in the infinite wisdom of God He came up with this marvelous plan of salvation.

- Righteousness -- we would have no hope of having the righteousness required to stand before God were it not that "we might be made the righteousness of God in Him" (2Cor. 5:21).

- Sanctification -- God set us apart that we might be His people (Titus 2:14).

- Redemption -- Only His blood could have purchased it (Eph. 1:7; 1Cor. 6:20).

[p] Verse 31 ("He that glorieth, let him glory in the Lord.") is quoted from Jeremiah 9:24 and repeated in 2Corinthians 10:17.

Annotations on 1Corinthians 2

Paul's preaching is of Christ crucified (a crucified Messiah). This is wisdom that imparts the wisdom of God.

"1 And I, brethren, when I came to you, came not with excellency of speech[a] or of wisdom, declaring unto you the testimony[b] of God. 2 For I determined not to know any thing among you, save Jesus Christ, and him crucified. 3 And I was with you in weakness[c], and in fear, and in much trembling. 4 And my speech[d] and my preaching *was* not with enticing words of man's wisdom, but in demonstration of the Spirit and of power: [5] That[e] your faith should not stand in the wisdom of men, but in the power of God." (1Cor. 2:1-5)

[a] The expression "excellency of speech or of wisdom" has reference to the superior air or manner that is adopted by a speaker who is seeking to appear superior to his hearers for the purpose of establishing credibility with them. Paul, however, relied upon the Power of God for his credibility.

[b] The word translated here "testimony" is also translated "mystery." Verses 2 through 5 talk about the testimony while Verses 6 through 10 of Chapter 2 are about the mystery. In saying "I determined," we understand that Paul disciplined himself not to go anywhere with the Corinthians in his doctrine but the cross until they were established in that truth.

[c] Reading the account in Acts 18:9, it is apparent that Paul's emotional state was low when he was at Corinth. He was there in:

- Weakness—bodily infirmity (sick)

- Fear—fear of personal injury

- Trembling—to tremble with anxiety

Paul's demeanor among the Corinthians was not a display of eloquence and self confidence (2Cor. 10:10).

[d] "My speech" (Verse 4) - that which he was saying and "My preaching"- that which he proclaimed publicly was not with enticing words. "Enticing" means persuasive. Paul's speech lacked any ability to persuade by means of clever arguments that might win acceptance by the appeal to the natural man. Paul was relying on the Holy Spirit to do the work of conversion by convincing his hearers and convicting them of sin (Rom 15:19; 1Thess. 1:5). Rather, Paul's preaching was in the demonstration of "the Spirit and of power." Paul had complete confidence that the simple message of the cross had the power to save souls and transform lives (Rom. 1:16).

[e] The reason Paul disciplined himself to avoid persuasive words of man's wisdom is so that the Corinthians might realize that the object of their faith was not just some temporal philosophy of human origin, but the power of God to actually accomplish salvation for them.

It was only to those of mature faith that Paul could impart God's wisdom

"[6] Howbeit[f] we speak wisdom among them that are perfect: yet not the wisdom[g] of this world, nor of the princes of this world, that come to nought: [7] But we speak the wisdom of God in a mystery[h], *even* the hidden *wisdom*, which God ordained before the world unto our glory: [8] Which none of the princes of this world[i] knew: for had they known *it*[j], they would not have crucified the Lord of glory[k]. [9] But as it is written[l], Eye hath not seen, nor ear heard, neither have entered into the heart of man, the things which God hath prepared for them that love him. [10] But God hath revealed *them*[m] unto us by his Spirit: for the Spirit searcheth[n] all things, yea, the deep things of God." (1Cor. 2:6-10)

[f] Though Paul would not move beyond the preaching of Christ crucified until the believer was established, Paul did move on to speaking a form of wisdom to the mature (i.e. the "perfect") believers (Gal. 5:16).

[g] In Verse 6 he talks about the wisdom of this world. "This world" is a reference to this age, as in Galatians 1:4. The wisdom of this world goes no where – it "comes to nought." The present rulers of this age will diminish and cease to rule one day (1Cor. 15:24). In contrast to any wisdom that this world has to offer, we speak the "wisdom of God" in a mystery (literally "we reveal a secret"). This is wisdom that was hidden from man until the time was right for it to be revealed. To make sure that we understand that the mystery in view here is not to mean something mysterious and hard to understand, but rather something that was kept secret, he adds the fact that it was "the hidden wisdom". Paul makes mention of the mystery here but does not elaborate on it. To clearly identify what the mystery is, we have to go to some of the other Pauline epistles. The mystery is the very subject of the epistle of Ephesians. There we find that the mystery is "the one new man" of Jew and Gentile (Eph. 2:15) made one in the church which is Christ's body (Eph. 5:32). It has to do with everything concerning that body: its beginning, how it is formed, what is its role today, and what its eternal destiny is, etc. The mystery was revealed through Paul (Eph. 3:2). It completed the Word of God (Col. 1:25-26) when it was added to the cannon of scripture, and it is what establishes believers today (Rom. 16:25).

[h] Verse 7 speaks of the wisdom of God in a mystery (lit. in a secret). God ordained before the world began that there would be a body of believers through whom He would reconcile the heavenly places back to Himself. We can logically presume from this that the defection of Satan and his angels took place before the world began and therefore God purposed that, whatever their place and function was, it would be replaced by that of the "church which is Christ's body" (Col. 1:15-23). It was ordained of God before the foundation of the world (Eph. 1:4) but was kept secret, "hid in God" (Eph. 3:9), "hid from ages and from generations" (Col. 1:26), but "now is made manifest to his saints." As far as any scripture written before Paul is concerned, you can search them all you want and you will not find a single trace of this mystery (secret) church. The reason for God ordaining the mystery is here given as being "unto our glory." That is, its revelation is unto the glory of the "church which is His body".

To understand **"the wisdom of God in a mystery"** that Paul talks about, we consider four attributes of God and how those attributes affect us His creatures. Those attributes are:

1. His infinite love for sinners by which He desires to have all men be able to love Him and enjoy Him forever.

2. His perfect holiness which compels Him to be separate from sin. This attribute would exclude all men from His presence because all men have sinned. This leaves God and man in a predicament because His love desires that we be with Him but His holiness forbids it.

3. His perfection in justice compels Him to punish every sin. This leaves us in an even greater predicament. Not only are we excluded from His presence by our sin but His justice demands that our sin be punished. Now we (and God) would have a great problem were it not for a fourth attribute of God – that being His infinite wisdom.

4. God's infinite wisdom is put on display in the preaching of the cross. The cross enabled God to bring us the sinners into His presence without bringing sin with us. In the person of the one who is both God and man in one person, Jesus Christ the only begotten Son of God, being fully God and fully man, could pay man's sin debt in full. He could do that because he was the only person who had no sin of His own to atone for. He could therefore pay sin's debt for every man. All who believe can therefore now come to God having the righ-

teousness of God imputed to their account while their sins were imputed to the Savior and thus be forgiven. This is the greatest display of wisdom that either men or angels have ever seen.

[i] Who are these princes which Verse 8 refers to? Daniel 10:13 gives us much information on this matter. The prince of the Kingdom of Persia withstood the one who appeared to Daniel (*see Daniel 10:5-6*) and he did it for 21 days. We see (in Dan. 10:13) that Michael is one of the chief princes (archangels) and that he is the prince of Israel. Just as surely as the holy angels are/were sent to minister salvation to the elect of Israel (Heb. 1:14) and to her Messiah (Dan. 7:10; Matt. 4:11; Mark 1:13), so the fallen angels are actively involved in supporting and upholding the world system (John 7:7; Matt. 4:8; Rev. 13:8) which rejects Christ. The word "world" in Matthew 4:8 means the organized masses of humanity united with the common desire to exclude God from their common culture. The word for "world" in 1Corinthians 2:6 & 8 is elsewhere translated "age." It depicts a period of time that is "evil" (Gal. 1:4). It is evil because it is dominated by Satan who is the god of it (2Cor. 4:4). In Ezekiel 28 we see God talking through the physical prince of Tyre to the spirit prince of Tyre (Ezek. 28:2, 12) who turns out to be Satan himself (Ezek. 28:12-19).

- See: Ezekiel 28:16 where he is "The covering cherub."

- Satan as the prince of this world (John 12:31; 14:30; 16:11).

- Contrast that with Christ as the prince of Life (Acts 3:5; 5:31).

[j] What was it that none of the princes of this world knew in Verse 8? It is the wisdom of God in a mystery or secret. The content of this mystery was kept secret from everyone but God Himself (Eph. 3:9). It was revealed by Jesus Christ to angels and men through Paul (Eph. 3:2-3). This Pauline revelation has two elements to it. First of all, what was really accomplished on the cross (i.e. redemption through His blood -- Rom. 3:25 & Eph. 1:7-9) was revealed first through Paul as the "mystery of [i.e. the key to] the gospel" (Eph. 6:20). This is what Paul calls "my gospel" (Rom. 16:25; 2:16). It was through Paul's gospel (i.e. the cross) that God could righteously remit sins that are past (i.e. in past dispensations) that were covered by the blood of bulls and goats (Heb. 9:11-15) through the forbearance of God (Rom. 3:25). This was the "gospel of God" onto which Paul was separated (Rom. 1:1). The second element of the Pauline revelation involves the calling out of the Church which is Christ's Body (Col. 1:24-27) as the agency by which he would reconcile the heavenly places (Eph. 1:3; *cf* 2Cor. 5:1-10; II Tim 2:10) back to Himself through Christ (Col. 1:15-20). These heavenly places are today in the hands of "the prince of the power of the air" (Eph. 2:2).

[k] The one who owns glory and who is the "Lord of glory" is the Lord Jesus Christ, for "all things were created by him and for him" (Col. 1:16). The glory that belongs to Christ in the earth was usurped by Satan (2Cor. 4:4; Matt. 4:8). So too, the glory that belonged to Christ in the heavens was usurped by this same creature of God (Isa. 14:12-17; Eph. 2:2). But the worst atrocity was when the incarnate Creator was put to death by his creatures (humans) under the direction of "the prince of this world" (John 14:30; *cf* 12:31; 16:11).

[l] Verse 10 is a quote from Isaiah 64:4 where we see an expression of the hope of the believing remnant of Israel. Let's consider that statement. It says that "since the beginning of the world" no one but God has heard or seen the things that God has prepared for those who wait in hope on Him. That can be said of the entire Old Testament. Paul then goes on to state in Verse 10 of 1Corinthians 2 that those things are now revealed to us. But we ask "What are those things?" For Israel in Old Testament times, it was not that God would reconcile the earth to Himself through

the coming Messiah for that was well testified of in the Old Testament scriptures. However, what was never revealed before (and now revealed through Paul) was the righteousness of God imputed to the believers of all dispensations via the cross and that God will reconcile everything in heaven and earth to Himself through believers (whether in Israel's program or in the Body of Christ) who have trusted in the blood of the cross or (for the Old Testament believers) -- the blood of the sacrifice that God required. Simply put, the things regarding redemption and the eternal blessings that go to God's people as a result of Calvary are now revealed in the Scriptures. This is the truth of Romans 3:24-26.

[m] "But God hath revealed them [i.e. the things which He hath prepared for them that love Him] unto us by his Spirit." But did not God reveal the mystery to Paul directly through Christ? Yes! Paul got his message "...not after man...neither was [he] taught it, but by the revelation of Jesus Christ" (Gal. 1:12). But this verse is talking about how we get this information. Paul wrote his message down and we have it in the same way that we have any revelation from God -- i.e. in the Holy Scriptures. All scripture is given by inspiration of God (2Tim. 3:16) as "holy men of God spoke as they were moved by the Holy Ghost" (2Peter 1:20-21). 1Peter 1:10-12 indicates that there were meanings couched in the words of Old Testament prophecies which could not be fully revealed until the time was right. It is the Holy Spirit who teaches the Word of God -- "in the words [i.e. the Holy Scriptures] which the Holy Ghost teaches; comparing spiritual things with spiritual" (1Cor. 2:13).

[n] The words "The Spirit searches all things" in Verse 10 means the Spirit investigates and explores all things. The Holy Spirit knows the deep things of God and, using the scriptures, teaches them to the believer. Paul illustrates the enlightening work of the Holy Spirit by reference to the human spirit in man. Man is a three part creature of spirit, soul and body (I Thess. 5:23). This is part of the "image of God" in which man was created (Gen. 1:26-27). It is the Soul that is the seat of emotions, that gives a man his unique identity (the unique person), and gives him self consciousness – a consciousness of his unique personality. The spirit of a man is that part of man that "knows." It is the spirit that gives a man God consciousness. In the natural man, that spirit is dead and dormant. The spirit in Adam was that part of Adam that died the moment that he sinned (Gen. 2:17). His physical death came some time later as a result of having the sin nature resident in his physical body (Rom. 8:10; Gen. 3:14). The human spirit in any given man is the only entity who knows the mind and thoughts of that particular man. So too, the spirits in men are the means by which men can communicate knowledge to each other. In a similar way, the things of God (i.e. the thoughts and mind of God) are known only by the Spirit of God who communicates to the spirit of a man as that man studies the Word of God.

> "11 For what man knoweth[o] the things of a man, save the spirit of man which is in him? even so the things of God knoweth no man, but the Spirit of God. 12 Now we have received, not the spirit of the world, but the spirit which is of God; that[p] we might know the things that are freely given to us of God. 13 Which things also we speak, not in the words which man›s wisdom[q] teacheth, but which the Holy Ghost teacheth; comparing spiritual things with spiritual." (1Cor. 2:11-13)

[o] The word "Knoweth" in Verse 11 is in the perfect tense. That is talking about knowledge that was previously acquired and, as a result, we continue to have. We (believers) once had the spirit of this world (Eph 2:2; 2Cor 4:4) but now we (believers) have received "the Spirit which is of God" -- the spirit of which God is the source. The spirit

of Satan dominates this age (2Cor. 4:4) and this world (1John 5:19). We do not, as believers, share that spirit of the world. We can adopt it in the sense of being worldly (Phil. 3:17-19) but our nature as believers is to tune into the things of God.

[p] The reason for our receiving the Spirit which comes from God is "that we might know" the things that are freely given to us of God. Which things [i.e. the things of God which no man knows but the Spirit of God] are the things we speak. (Paul has been using the first person plural pronoun since Verse 1). He includes us as we teach the Pauline epistles.

[q] We do not speak the things of God in the human logic that is used to teach secular concepts. Instead, we use words which the Holy Ghost uses. Secular psychology and secular philosophy (and economics and sociology and even secular theology) will never communicate spiritual truth. Only the Holy Spirit can do that. He does that through the Word. "Comparing spiritual things with spiritual" literally means using spiritual means (words which the Holy Ghost teaches from the Bible) to communicate spiritual concepts (i.e. the things of God).

The natural man does not understand the things of God

> "[14] But the natural man[r] receiveth not the things of the Spirit of God: for they are foolishness unto him: neither can he know *them*, because they are spiritually discerned. [15] But he that is spiritual[s] judgeth[t] all things, yet he himself is judged of no man. [16] For who hath known the mind of the Lord, that he may instruct him? But we have the mind of Christ." (1Cor. 2:14-16)

[r] "The natural man" is literally the soulish man. It is the man the way he is born into this world; having a dormant spirit and focused on the soul -- the self (he is self-centered rather than God-centered). It is the spirit in the three part makeup of man that is designed by God to tune in to the things of God. This is the part of man that died when Adam sinned (*see note [n]*). Before it can function as God intended it to, it must be "regenerated" (Titus 3:5). The natural man's indifference to God is summarized thus:

- He receives not the things of the Spirit of God (i.e. the Word of God which He has revealed through the Spirit).

- The things of God are foolishness to him.

- He can not know them. The reason that he has no power or ability to know them is "because they are spiritually discerned." He needs a quickened spirit to understand them. This quickening of the spirit is done by God when the sinner hears the gospel and believes it (Titus 3:5).

[s] Here, in Verse 15 and in the verses that follow, Paul lists the second of four different kinds of men. The four kinds of men are:

- The Natural man -- an unbeliever or an unregenerate man.

- He that is Spiritual -- a believer who focuses on the things of God and the hereafter.

- Carnal—a believer who focuses on self and the here and now.

- Babes—a new believer

He that is spiritual is a believer who is tuned in to the Word of God and therefore thinks the way Christ thinks and therefore has the mind of Christ. The written Word is the mind of the living Word – the word of Christ. He is not only "tuned in" to the Word, he is also focused on the things of the Word -- the unseen eternal things (2Cor. 4:18).

[t] The words "judges" and "judged" in Verse 16 here is the same word rendered "discerned" in the previous verse. The spiritual person has the ability to discern and critically examine (accurately) all things that are going on around him—being fully instructed out of the Word.

Annotations on 1Corinthians 3
The Corinthian saints were not ready for the solid food of Paul's teaching

"[1] And I, brethren[a], could not speak unto you as unto spiritual, but as unto carnal[b], *even* as unto babes[c] in Christ. [2] I have fed you with milk[d], and not with meat: for hitherto ye were not able *to bear it*, neither yet now are ye able. [3] For ye are yet carnal: for whereas *there is* among you envying[e], and strife, and divisions, are ye not carnal, and walk[f] as men? [4] For while one saith[g], I am of Paul; and another, I *am* of Apollos; are ye not carnal?" (1Cor. 3:1-4)

[a] Note Paul's address: "I, brethren." Paul, before pointing out the carnality of the Corinthians, refers to them as "brethren." Paul was ever-sensitive to where people are "at" spiritually and tailored his teaching of spiritual things to their level of maturity. This kind of sensitivity is necessary in anyone who ministers the Word if he is to be effective. To bore the spiritually mature with the fundamentals and to inundate the spiritually immature with material they cannot handle are both futile efforts. Paul could not give them the spiritual meat that he alluded to in 1Corinthians 2:6-8.

[b] Our English word "carnal" comes from the Latin and Spanish words for "meat" or "flesh." The term as used here has reference to the believer who will not see beyond the physical body and the here and now. These Corinthians were no longer "natural" men because they, having trusted Jesus Christ as Savior, were all regenerated. So too, they are no longer babes because they had been believers for some five years by the time of the writing of 1Corinthians. They had all of the resources that they needed to live their Christian life on a spiritual plane -- focused on the things of God (the things that are not seen). The sad fact is that they had no excuse for their immaturity. In this present evil age while we anguish under the curse of Genesis 3, it is possible to find physical bodies that are stunted and minds that are retarded. However, in the giving of the new life to the believer, God gave each believer all the resources that he or she needed to grow to full spiritual maturity. If the believer would only tune into the things of God and be instructed from the Word of God (rightly divided), he would have the mind of Christ. The tragedy of the situation at Corinth is that most of the believers were not availing themselves to these spiritual resources.

The question might be raised here: "Is the old sin nature that produces carnality in the believer attached to the physical body?" In Romans 7:16 Paul says "for I know that in me (that is in my flesh) dwelleth no good thing..." It is through his physical body though that the sin nature operates. For the believer, God performed a spiritual surgery -- a spiritual circumcision (Colossians 2:10-12) to separate him/her from the old sin nature so that the believer can live a life without sin's dominion. This is the work of God described in Romans 6:1-10. This is a special work of God that is unique to His working in the Church which is Christ's Body. Only the apostle Paul describes this work of

God because it is the working of the Gospel of the Grace of God that was revealed through him. The believer today needs only two things to live his life on a spiritual plane:

The first being "That form of doctrine which was delivered you" (i.e. Pauline doctrine) and

The second being obedience "from the heart" to that form of doctrine (Rom. 6:17).

[c] The term "Babes" means non speakers. These Corinthians were in the same state as the Hebrews (see Hebrews 5:11-14). Paul was, as all effective Bible teachers are, sensitive to and acutely interested in where people are at spiritually. He, having determined that the Corinthians were at the "babes" stage spiritually, tailored his teaching to deal with them at that level. Because of their state, he could not speak to them as to spiritual. It was not that Paul would not speak to them as unto spiritual, but that he could not do so. They would not be able to handle it.

[d] What was the milk? Or perhaps a better question is, "what was the meat that he couldn't feed the Corinthians?" The answer to that is evident in the canonical order of the Pauline epistles. The book of Romans contains the basic doctrine that every believer needs as foundational information to successfully live under grace. The Corinthian epistles are then reproof for carnality. The Galatians epistle is correction for bad doctrine. Then Ephesians comes along with instruction in righteousness concerning the believer's walk having all-spiritual blessings in heavenly places in Christ. 2Timothy 3:16 lays out this pattern also. Ephesians, Philippians, and Colossians contain "the wisdom of God in a mystery" which Paul told the Corinthians, that he spoke to "them that are perfect [mature]" (1Corinthians 2:6-7). We understand then that "Meat" in Verse 2 means "solid food".

[e] In Verse 3 Paul says "Ye are yet carnal", and the evidence is that there was among them:

- **Envying** - to nurse an attitude of envy toward one another. One who truly understands the concept of the one body would rejoice over the good fortune and grace of God bestowed on another.

- **Strife** - quarreling and contention between believers in the assembly. Such an attitude was manifested as a failure to recognize the truth of Romans Chapter 6 regarding the walk after the Spirit. The individual believer involved is letting Sin (the sin nature) run his/her affairs. Before they could go on to advanced truth, they need to get a handle on this basic truth.

- **Divisions** - standing apart. Paul warned of people who would cause such division in Romans 16:17.

[f].The natural man is in view here in Verse 3 and in 2:16 with the comment of walking as men. The believer is a man in whom something supernatural happens by virtue of the process of regeneration. He can, as a regenerate man, "walk worthy of the vocation wherewith he was called" (Eph. 4:1). Here though, we see believers walking as unregenerate men walk (see Eph. 2:2-3 on how the lost walk).

[g] The evidence of carnality was given in Verse 3. Here in Verse 4, we have a manifestation of carnality -- that being sectarianism. The Corinthians were picturing Paul and Apollos as leaders of different sects. The carnal mind cannot picture men working together for the good of the whole. The cure for carnality is a heart surrendered to God as stated in Romans 6:17 ("But God be thanked, that ye were the servants of sin, but ye have obeyed from the heart that form of doctrine which was delivered you."). Then, once surrendered, the believer can rejoice in the heart attitude of Galatians 2:20 "I am crucified with Christ: nevertheless I live; yet not I, but Christ liveth in me: and the life which

I now live in the flesh I live by the faith of the Son of God, who loved me, and gave himself for me." Until a believer gets a handle on the doctrine of Romans Chapters 6-8, he/she cannot move on to advanced truth.

The More Excellent Way – Faith, Hope and Love

"[1] Though I speak with the tongues of men and of angels, and have not charity[a], I am become *as* sounding brass, or a tinkling cymbal. [2] And though I have *the gift of* prophecy, and understand all mysteries, and all knowledge; and though I have all faith, so that I could remove mountains, and have not charity, I am nothing. [3] And though I bestow all my goods to feed *the poor*, and though I give my body to be burned, and have not charity, it profiteth me nothing. [4] Charity[b] suffereth long, *and* is kind; charity envieth not; charity vaunteth not itself, is not puffed up, [5] Doth not behave itself unseemly, seeketh not her own, is not easily provoked, thinketh no evil; [6] Rejoiceth not in iniquity, but rejoiceth in the truth; [7] Beareth all things, believeth all things, hopeth all things, endureth all things. [8] Charity never faileth[c]: but whether *there be* prophecies, they shall fail; whether *there be* tongues, they shall cease; whether *there be* knowledge, it shall vanish away." (1Cor. 13:1-8) (1Corinthians 13:1-8)

[a] Verses 1 thru 3 makes a powerful statement that one can posses the greatest of gifts but if he is lacking charity he is nothing. The word translated charity is the word for love that is freely bestowed without there being a quality in the one loved that compels such love. Such love can only come as the outgrowth of grace in the heart of the believer. It is the work of the Holy Spirit in the believer that produces such love.

[b] In Verses 4 thru 7 the apostle tells us what charity does (how it acts). What should occur to the Corinthians is that, based on the preceding chapters of this epistle, it is apparent that they were not doing these things.

[c] In Verse 8 the apostle makes the point on the endurance of existence of the gifts listed in this chapter. The gift of charity never fails and will never cease to exist (as we see in Verse 13) – it never ceases to function. This was written in 59 A.D. What is significant in this passage is that there is coming a time (post 59 AD) when prophecies (as a supernatural gift) will fail. Also, the gift of tongues will cease to exist. So too knowledge (the ability to know things by supernatural means) will vanish away. However charity will never fail – it will never cease to function.

The Body of Christ in Adulthood

"[9] For we know in part, and we prophesy in part. [10] But when[d] that which is perfect is come, then that which is in part shall be done away. [11] When I was a child[e] I spake as a child, I understood as a child, I thought as a child: but when I became a man, I put away childish things. [12] For now we see through a glass, darkly; but then face to face: now I know in part; but then shall I know even as also I am known. [13] And now abideth faith, hope, charity, these three; but the greatest of these *is* charity." (1Cor. 13:9-13)

[d] We saw in note [c] above that the gift of tongues will cease, the gift of knowledge will vanish, the gift of prophecy will fail. The question is "when will this happen?" It must be remembered that Verse 9 was written in 59 AD Verse 9 says that at that time the church had partial knowledge and partial prophecy (now being in 59 AD when this was written) we know in part and prophesy in part. Verse 10 then looks to a time when that which is perfect is come. The word translated "perfect" is the word for completeness. Considering the context, we understand "that which is perfect" is the completion of "that which is in part" in Verse 10. That would be prophesy, and knowledge. In 59 AD the church prophesied in part and knew God's plan for the ages in part. The "now" of Verse 12 is the time when the church saw "through a glass darkly." The "then" of Verse 12 is referring to the time when the church will "know even as it is known." The illustration of the glass is to the polished metal used for a mirror in those days. One's reflection in such a mirror was probably fuzzy at best. That was what the church's view of the knowledge of God's plan for the ages was at that time. However, when full knowledge and full prophecy is come, then the image will be clear like one was looking face to face. The full knowledge and the full prophecy came with the completion of the cannon of scripture. Once the Bible was complete, anything to do with the childhood of the church vanished and ceased. Now with the completed Word of God, the man of God is fully equipped and thoroughly furnished onto every good work (2Tim. 3:16)

[e] In Verse 11, the apostle draws another illustration – that of a child's knowledge of life in comparison with the adult's knowledge. During the period covered by the Book of Acts the church which is Christ's body was in its infancy and childhood. It was then that God dealt with the church by means of supernatural gifts of the Spirit to equip the church to function before the full revelation of the word of God was given. See Ephesians 4:8-15 on what the adulthood of the Body of Christ is like. We as believers today have the resources in the completed Word of God to live our lives on the spiritual plane of spiritual mature adults in the family of God.

Wisdom in Decision Making

As parents, we will be called upon by our children to offer wise advice on decision making. When called upon for such wise counsel, we do need to be clear ourselves on what the will of God is regarding the process of making decisions in life. Before getting into decision making, we need to be sure that we ourselves understand the will of God so as to give counsel to our children. Let's therefore do a Bible study on the will of God in general. We will address the subject by considering what the Bible has to say about each of three wills that God might have that affects our lives. We will start with the question "Does God have three wills?"

Much of Christianity today holds the view that God has not only a sovereign will and a moral will (both of which He clearly does have), but that He also has an individual will for each believer. This "individual will" would be a unique plan (a specific life map) specifically designed by God for each person. This view (that God has an individual will) then holds that each person has to somehow "read the tea leaves" to try to figure out what that individual will that God has for their life is. The individual then would have to follow the road signs to ascertain this individual will of God for their personal lives. The road signs would then be construed to include: the Bible, inner impressions, personal desire, the circumstances of life, counsel from pastors, parents, or some special guidance as for example putting out a fleece. The problem with this is that all of these except the Bible are subjective measures and can not be verified as authoritative as being from God.

The material in the following three pages has been gleaned in summary from the book *"Decision making and the Will of God."* Moltnomah Press

God has a Sovereign Will

We do know that God has a sovereign will. His sovereign will is connected with His eternal purpose for His creation. Actually, His eternal purpose is two fold. He has a purpose for the earth and He has a purpose for the heavens. His sovereign will encompasses both the heaven and the earth. His eternal purpose for the earth centers in Bible Prophecy and the nation of Israel. His eternal purpose for the heavens centers in the body of doctrine that the apostle Paul calls the preaching of Jesus Christ according to the revelation of the mystery and focuses on the church the Body of Christ.

We see the surety of God's sovereign will connected with his purpose for the earth in Isaiah 14:24-27.

> "²⁴ The LORD of hosts hath sworn, saying, Surely as I have thought, so shall it come to pass; and as I have purposed, *so* shall it stand: ²⁵ That I will break the Assyrian in my land, and upon my mountains tread him under foot: then shall his yoke depart from off them, and his burden depart from off their shoulders. ²⁶ This *is* the purpose that is purposed upon the whole earth: and this *is* the hand that is stretched out upon all the nations. ²⁷ For the LORD of hosts hath purposed, and who shall disannul *it*? and his hand *is* stretched out, and who shall turn it back?

The Assyrian in this passage is the antichrist. The purpose that God has in Bible Prophecy is to break the antichrist's grip on the earth and to set up His Kingdom.

We see the eternal purpose for the heavens in the Pauline epistles in which we see God setting His focus on the heavenly places. His will for the heavens is contained in the mystery revealed through Paul. This body of doctrine presents to us the eternal purpose for the heavens. This eternal purpose is centered in the church the Body of Christ. Paul talks about that eternal purpose in Ephesians 3:9-11

> "⁹ And to make all *men* see what *is* the fellowship of the mystery, which from the beginning of the world hath been hid in God, who created all things by Jesus Christ: ¹⁰ To the intent that now unto the principalities and powers in heavenly *places* might be known by the church the manifold wisdom of God, ¹¹ According to the eternal purpose which he purposed in Christ Jesus our Lord:..."

In God's sovereign will, He makes all of the decisions and He takes all of the actions. Our part in His sovereign will is simply that we need to know what His sovereign will is. This sovereign will involving His eternal purpose is entirely connected with the unfolding of the dispensations of God (Col. 1:25; Eph. 3:1-10). He devised His eternal purpose for the heavens "Before the foundation of the world" (John 17:24; Eph. 1:4; 1Peter 1:20). His eternal purpose for the earth was formulated by Him "from the foundation of the world" (Matt. 13:35; 25:34; Heb. 4:3; 9:16). God reveals His sovereign will as He unfolds it in history (1Cor. 2:6-8; Romans 16:25; Eph. 3:1).

God has a Moral Will for Man

God also has a moral will for man (Romans 12: 1 and 2). This moral will is the expression of His holy character in behavioral terms. It touches on every aspect of our human lives. It is fully revealed to every man in the Bible (2Tim. 3: 16 and 17). There are three aspects to the moral will in our lives: 1) Actions that we take – what we do (the product) 2) the Attitudes that we hold – why we do what we do (the purpose for our actions); and 3) the approach that we take – how we do it (the process).

But, does God have an Individual Will for Man?

As we study the scripture, we are lead to conclude that God does not have a specific individual will in the **normal course** of events for our lives. Here is where the freedom of sonship comes into play in the believer's life. I say "normal course" because God did have an individual will for certain individuals at certain times. Noah, Abraham, Joseph, Pharaoh, Moses, David, Jonah and Paul are all examples of these exceptions to the normal. These exceptions always involved supernatural intervention in the normal affairs of life. This was only in events connected with changes in human history involved with God's sovereign will being carried out. These interventions are usually involved in dispensational changes in God's dealings with man. This intervention was always the exception and not the rule.

Let's consider the example of Paul. God had a specific will for his life in connection with his conversion (Acts 9:3-4 cf. Gal. 1:1; and 1Cor. 1:1), when he was commissioned (Acts 13:1-2), and when God gave him special direction (Acts 16:6-10; 18:9-10; 22:17-21; 23:11; etc.). However, most of the time, Paul was left to decide on his course of action for himself (Acts 15:36; 20:16; Romans 1:10-13; 1Cor. 16:4-9; 2Cor. 1:15-20; etc.).

Bible Based Principles for Decision Making

God's Word does not tell us individually what to decide in every situation but it does teach us how to come to a wise decision that is acceptable to God. The Bible:

1. Fully reveals God's moral will.

2. Provides us the knowledge of God's sovereign will which reveal His goals and purposes (Eph. 1:10; Isa. 14:20).

3. Gives us the wisdom of how to apply that knowledge (Eph. 1:17; Col. 1:9).

4. Tells us what God's involvement in our spiritual lives really is (Romans Chapters 6 through 8).

5. Gives us the objective standard by which we may define and recognize what is moral and wise.

6. Defines for us our human makeup (Heb. 4:12).

7. The Bible functions as an indicator to tell us when we are off track (Gal. 5:18-22).

A decision is acceptable to God if:

1. It is consistent with the explicit commands of scripture rightly divided (1Thess. 4:1-3).

2. It is consistent with the goals and purposes of God as revealed in His Word. The believer's goals in order to be consistent with God's goals should:

- Glorify God in all things – every thought, word, and action (1Cor. 10:23; Romans 14:19).

- Fulfill our God ordained responsibilities (Eph. 5:22-6:9-10).

- Reach lost people with the gospel (1Cor. 10:3; 2Peter 3:9; 1Tim. 2:4).

- Bear the fruit of righteousness (1Cor. 6:12; Eph. 2:12; Col. 1:10).

How do we acquire wisdom for those non-moral decisions?

1. We need to have the right attitude:

- Be humble – willingly recognize that you do not know everything (Proverbs 11:25; Philippians 2:5-8).

- Be teachable – The one who knows everything can not learn anything (Proverbs 9:9; 15:31; 19:20).

- Do your research (Proverbs 8:17 cf. 2: 4&5; Col. 3:23).

- Resolve to be upfront and upright in all of your dealings (Proverbs 2:7).

- Have reverence for God and His will (Proverbs 9:10).

2. We need to take the right approach:

- Seek wisdom from the pages of Scripture (2Tim. 2:7; 3:15-17).

- Seek wisdom from wise counsel.

- Seek wisdom from the experience of life – learn from past mistakes and from those of others.

- Pray for wisdom (Col. 1:9-10).

The exercise of trying to find an individual will of God when such a will dose not exist leads to frustration and to ignorant and immature decisions being made. This leads to frustration by:

- Permitting believers to justify unwise decisions on the grounds that "God told me to do it."

- By permitting costly delays in making a decision while people are "reading the road signs."

- By encouraging the practice of "putting out a fleece" and thus letting the circumstances dictate the decision.

There are many good reasons to reject inner impressions as direction from God in decision making. They include:

1. Scripture says nothing about the Holy Spirit leading believers through inner impressions.

2. We can't be certain of the source of the inner impressions.

3. We can't be certain of the message that the inner impressions would be trying to convey.

4. Some other verification would be needed in order for inner impressions to be authoritative.

5. There is no authority in such impressions to compel obedience.

How then should we respond to inner impressions? We should:

1. Recognize that they can come from a number of sources of which none can be verified as being from God.

2. Recognize that they do not represent divine guidance.

3. Recognize that they must be judged on the authority of the Word of God.

To summarize the basic principles of Wise Decision Making:

1. In those areas specifically addressed in the Bible, the revealed commands of God are to be obeyed. They represent God's moral will.

2. In those areas where the Bible gives no command or principle, the believer is free to choose his/her own course of action. Any decision made within the moral will of God is acceptable to God.

In those non-moral decisions the believer should have as his/her objective to make wise decisions on the basis of what is most spiritually profitable in the context of eternity (that is -- to make decisions with eternity in view).

CHAPTER 9
THE LOVE AND REVERENCE LINK
TO SUCCESS IN MARRIAGE

The Marriage Compact

Ephesians 5:21

21 Submitting yourselves one to another in the fear of God.

The fear of God in Verse 21 is the sphere in which believers submit themselves to one another. The term "in the fear of God" recognizes that the authority structure that exists for the proper functioning of society does so under the authority of God. It also carries the idea that we will each be accountable as to how we have each filled our God-ordained roles in that structure and framework.

Ephesians 5:22-33

"22 Wives, submit[a] yourselves unto your own husbands, as unto the Lord. 23 For the husband is the head[b] of the wife, even as Christ is the head of the church: and he is the saviour of the body. 4 Therefore as the church is subject unto Christ, so *let* the wives *be* to their own husbands in every thing[c]. 25 Husbands, love your wives, even as Christ also loved[d] the church, and gave himself for it: 26 That he might sanctify and cleanse it with the washing of water by the word, 27 That he might present[e] it to himself a glorious church, not having spot, or wrinkle, or any such thing; but that it should be holy and without blemish. 28 So ought men to love their wives as their own bodies. He that loveth his wife loveth himself. 29 For no man ever yet hated his own flesh; but nourisheth and cherisheth it, even as the Lord the church: 30 For we are members of his body, of his flesh, and of his bones. 31 For this cause[f] shall a man leave his father and mother, and shall be joined unto his wife, and they two shall be one flesh. 32 This is a great mystery: but I speak concerning Christ and the church. 33 Nevertheless let every one of you in particular so love[g] his wife even as himself; and the wife *see* that she reverence *her* husband." (Eph. 5:22-33)

[a] Wives are to "submit" unto their own husbands; It does not say "obey" as children are admonished to in Verse 6:11. The word "submit" means to recognize order and authority for the purpose of peace and harmony. Wives are to submit to "their own" husbands. The submission here is not a societal submission of women to men but here it is in the context of the marriage relationship.

In 1Timothy 2:11-14, the submission is in the context of the local church. There is a two-fold reason for such submission of women to men in the church:

- Adam was created first, then Eve.

- Adam was not deceived but Eve was.

Because "Adam was not deceived," we understand that the headship responsibility was his, but also the blame for the fall of mankind goes to him (Romans 5:14; 1Corinthians 15:22).

Paul addresses the principle of submission of the woman to the man in the local church again in I Corinthians 11:7-16. The fleshly mind rebels at the very thought but the Spirit still makes bold to say, "...the head of the woman is the man" (1Corinthians 11:3) and the Spirit filled woman would have it no other way. Note: In Genesis 2:7 we see that God created Adam's soul and spirit and then formed a body for Adam out of dust, then breathed into his nostrils the breath of life and man became a living soul. Then in Genesis 2:22-23, we see God taking Eve (the woman) out of man (Adam). In Genesis 2:24, we see the two of them becoming "one flesh". As "one flesh", there cannot be two heads. The woman was not created separately from Adam but was taken out of the man. As a result, there is only one human race and one head of the human race therefore there needs to be only one Redeemer. Jesus Christ the creator of the human race is the redeemer.

Wives are instructed in Verse 22 to submit to their own husbands as unto the Lord. That is, in the same manner as they would submit unto the Lord, they are to submit to their own husbands. The degree of submission would be tempered according to the principle of Acts 4:19 if the moral issue of the situation need so be.

[b] The doctrine of Christ's headship to the church is central to Paul's epistles (Ephesians 1:22, 4:15, 5:23; Colossians 1:18, 2:19). The very truth of the one body is the mystery (1Corinthians 2:10; Galatians 1:12; Ephesians 3:2-3). Paul's teaching of the "one new man" (Ephesians 2:15; Colossians 3:9) involves Christ as the head and the church of this dispensation composing the Body (Ephesians 1:22, 4:15, 5:23, 29; Colossians 1:18, 24, 2:29). The responsibility of headship is illustrated in Verses 23 & 25 as Paul presents Christ's work in headship as an example. Headship involves provision and protection (Verse 23). It also involves self-sacrifice as Christ "gave himself" for the church.

[c] Wives are to be subject to their own husbands "in everything." That means in every aspect of life. Does that mean that the wife is not morally responsible if her husband would have her involved in something which is opposed to God's Word? Acts 4:19 answers that: Men (and women) must obey God rather than to obey men.

Husbands are here given instruction on what their wives need more than anything else from their husbands -- that being love. This love is the unconditional "agape" love. It is the no-strings-attached love, unlike the love of which the world speaks, this love is a giving love. The passage in 1Corinthians 13:4-7 describes this kind of love. This love is a genuine charity -- free will distribution to the poor and needy. This love: suffers long, is kind, envieth not, is not jealous ... hopeth all things, endureth all things, and above all, this love never fails. Perhaps the greatest thing a man can do for his children is to love their mother with this kind of love.

[d] The example of the love husbands ought to have for their wives is Christ's love for the church. Simply put, Christ's love for the church is demonstrated in that He gave Himself for it that He might provide all of the needs of the church. The needs which the church had and which Christ provided are:

- Redemption: This need was satisfied by Christ giving himself in sacrifice for their sins. (Ephesians 5:1)

- Sanctification: This need was satisfied by Christ choosing the church "before the foundation of the world that we should be holy and without blame before him" (Ephesians 1:4).

- Cleansing: This need is met by the work of the Holy Spirit in the washing of the stain of sin as 1Corinthians 6:11 states

- Reconciliation: The church (speaking individually) had to be reconciled back to the creator. This Christ provided and will one day present it corporately to Himself without spot or wrinkle or any such thing...but that it might be holy and without blame. This encompasses both the imputed righteousness (2Cor. 5:21) and the life changing effect of the gospel of grace (Titus 2:12)

Christ loved the church before it was holy and without blemish. This goes back to Romans 5:8, "But God commendeth his love for us in that while we were yet sinners, Christ died for us". The expression "that he might sanctify it" is in the perfect tense and passive voice, indicating that Christ did all of the work to accomplish this. It also means that the result is that we are now holy as a result of His work on our behalf. As 1Corinthians 1:30 states, "Christ is made unto us wisdom and righteousness and sanctification and redemption".

The expression "and cleanse it by the washing of water by the word" is apparently to be taken as a figure of speech since the Word does not wash with water but it does wash from sin. The figure of speech is that of removing uncleanness by bathing. The spiritual application is using the Word as the means of cleansing. But note that this is a past tense action (the aorist tense). Christ has provided the means of cleansing in the past. 1Corinthians 6:11 uses the same figure of speech when it says, "and such were some of you; but ye are washed..." The word "washed" in 1Corinthians 6:11 is in the middle voice. That is action in which the subject is acting on himself. You did not provide the means of cleansing but you (the believer) did come to it and wash yourself in that which Christ provided -- that being the word.

[e] Husbands can not do for their wives what Christ did for the Church. Christ has provided all of that for their wives. What husbands are to do for their wives is to love them as Christ loved the church in providing for their physical, emotional, and spiritual needs. They are to give themselves as Christ gave Himself. That would mean that husbands are to give themselves to the point of death for their wives. This is an awesome responsibility but it is the manifestation of the Spirit in the lives of husbands.

Paul here relates the marriage relationship (that of husband and wife being one flesh) to the one new man of Ephesians 2:15. The one new man is Christ according to the revelation of the mystery -- that special and unique relation of Christ the head (Ephesians 1:22, 4:15, 5:23; Colossians 1:18, 2:19) together with the church which is his body (Ephesians 5:23 and 30; Colossians 1:24). There are two different types here. One type is the care which a person has for his/her own body. Just as we naturally take care of our own physical bodies, so Christ has such a natural concern for the church which is His body. The truth of that one body is the central theme of Paul's epistles. He speaks of it first in Romans 12:5. It is formed by the baptizing work of the Holy Spirit (1Corinthians 12:13). In fact, the union of head and body comprise the new creature of 2CorInthians 5:17 and Galatians 6:15.

[f] This passage (Ephesians 5:31) goes back to Genesis 2:24 where we find the law of marriage. The Lord refers to this in Matthew 19:5 and 6 where he adds, "...what therefore God hath joined together, let no man put asunder." God joins two believers together when they marry. When a man and woman marry in the Lord, they are regarded by God as one flesh for the purposes of the affairs of this life. This law of marriage is the law which Paul refers to in Romans 7:12 and 1Corinthians 7:39 when he says "the wife is bound by the law as long as her husband liveth; but if her husband be dead, she is at liberty to be married to whom she will." This law goes back before the Law of Moses. The Law of Moses is done away for us members of the Body (Colossians 2:14). However, the law of marriage for two believers joined in marriage remains as in Genesis 2:24

[g] The word "reverence" in Verse 33 is translated "fear" in Verse 21. Love and fear are here joined together. The wife's submission to the husband ought to be prompted by the husband's love for the wife as the church's submission unto Christ is prompted by Christ's love for the church (2Corinthians 5:14; Titus 2:4). Reverence is not the same thing as respect. Respect must be earned. Reverence however is something given because of the position that the one reverenced occupies. One of the greatest things a wife can do for her husband is to show this reverence toward her husband.

Stop the Crazy Cycle

Verse 33 is the key to making marriage work. I dare to say that if every husband and every wife fully applied the principle spelled out in this passage, there would be no divorce in America. It defines in one verse what every husband needs and can not function without (reverence) and what every wife needs and can not function without (love). There is an excellent reference work on marriage entitled "Love and Respect" by Dr. Emerson Eggerich. I recommend the book to anyone who offers counsel on marriage. The book is published by Thomas Nelson (ISBN 978-1-59145-187-7) It is also available with a DVD (ISBN 978-1-59145-417-5). In it he describes what he calls the crazy cycle. Every married couple can probably relate to this. In this crazy cycle, the husband withholds love (or vice versa – the wife disrespects here husband) and the wife responds saying in her heart "If he is not going to love me, I am not going to treat him with respect." He then in turn saying is his heart "How can a man love a woman who disrespects him as she does me?" And he all the more withholds his love and the cycle continues over and over again. It will continue until one or both of them stop to realize that this was not what God had in mind for marriage and they put the doctrine of love and respect (the basic doctrine of grace) into practice.

CHAPTER 10
THE FELLOWSHIP FACTOR IN MARRIAGE, FAMILY AND COMMUNITY

The Pillar and Ground of the Truth

The local church and the importance it plays in the life of the Spirit filled home is understood by the sequence: Sound Doctrine produces Strong Saints who maintain Strong Marriages who raise Strong Families who support Strong Churches which hold forth Sound Doctrine (1Tim. 3:15-16) which produces Strong Saints...and so on ad infinitum.

> **1 Timothy 3:14-16 (KJV)** "[14] These[a] things write I unto thee, hoping to come unto thee shortly: [15] But if I tarry long, that thou mayest know how thou oughtest to behave thyself in the house of God, which is the church of the living God, the pillar and ground of the truth. [16] And without controversy great is the mystery[b] of godliness: God was manifest in the flesh, justified in the Spirit, seen of angels, preached unto the Gentiles, believed on in the world, received up into glory."

God Manifest in the Flesh

[a] The reason for the writing of 1Timothy is given in Verses 14 thru 16: "that thou mayest know how thou oughtest to behave thyself in the house of God, which is the church of the living God...." Here "the house of God" is said to be the "church of the living God." This is not a building built of brick and stone, but rather a living "called out assembly" in which the "living God" dwells in the world. The local assembly is in view here. Everything that can be said about the "church which is Christ's body" at large can also be said of the local assembly. The Body of Christ, working through the local assembly is the pillar and ground of the truth. It is the means whereby truth, the only truth for today, is maintained in planet earth. In Verse 16, it (i.e. the house of God -- the church of the living God) is said to be the "mystery of godliness." The term "godliness" is the term for "good worship" in the Greek. The English term "godliness" is a compressed form of "God-like-ness." That is true worship when God's character and personality is lived out in the lives of believers. Besides being the "pillar and ground of the truth." the church is today the only viable means by which God can be properly worshipped in the world today. When the church is raptured from the earth (1Thess. 4:13-18), the world will be given up to "believe a lie" for then the pillar and ground of the truth will be gone. As a result, the world will be taking "pleasure in unrighteousness" (2 Thess. 2:10-12) rather than godliness.

[b] The "mystery of godliness" (that of good worship in the church) is defined as:

- **God "manifest in the flesh" in the church.** We were once manifesting Satan's character (Eph 2:2 & 2 Cor 4:4). Now God's character is or should be manifested in the justified sinner through regeneration and sanctification.

- **God was "justified in the Spirit".** The work of the Spirit in baptizing the believing sinner into Christ to transfer the sinner's guilt to Christ and Christ's righteousness to the sinner (2Cor. 5:21), enables God to "be just and [at the same time] the justifier of him which believes in Jesus" (Rom. 3:25).

- **Seen of Angels.** Christ defeated Satan on the cross: "...having spoiled principalities and powers [those in heavenly places of 1:16] he made a shew of them openly, triumphing over them in it [i.e. in the cross]" (Col 3:15). This is what Paul has referenced to in Ephesians 4:8 when he "led captivity captive." The captivity that he led captive (as a victorious army would lead its captive enemy captive in a victory parade) are the defeated principalities and powers in heavenly places. So too, as the victor over these defeated enemies, he "gave gifts to men." These gifts are for the equipping of the church to occupy the territory won and are in fact (ultimately) positions of responsibility in the world to come. Angels (both the elect and the fallen angels) are today watching this marvelous thing that God is doing in the earth in calling out the Body of Christ with its heavenly hope, heavenly calling, and heavenly destiny. In Ephesians 3:9, the church of this dispensation is said to be "the fellowship of the mystery which from the beginning of the world hath been hid in God, who created all things by Jesus Christ." And, God has now revealed it "to the intent <u>that now unto the principalities and powers in heavenly places might be known by the church the manifold wisdom of God</u>" (Eph 3:10).

- **Preached unto the Gentiles.** Paul's ministry was to reveal to the world the victory that was won by Christ on Calvary and the calling out of the body of believers that Christ is preparing to reign with him and to live there for His glory in the heavens. Note his words in Ephesians 3: "If ye have heard of the dispensation of the grace of God which is given me to youward...Unto me who am less than the least of all saints is this grace given, that <u>I should preach amoung the Gentiles the unsearchable riches of Christ...</u>" (Eph 3:2 & 8). God's program through Israel would eventually have reached the Gentiles through Israel's rising (Isa. 60:3; Rom. 15:9) were it not interrupted by the dispensation of grace. It will ultimately reach the Gentiles in the Kingdom. However, today, God is sending salvation to the Gentiles through Israel's fall (Rom. 11:11).

- **Believed on in the world.** God's last word to Israel before switching His dispensational dealings from Israel to the Gentiles is: "Be it known unto you, that the salvation of God is sent unto the Gentiles, and that they will hear it" (Acts 28:26).

- **Received up into glory.** This has reference to the future rapture of the church. It is presented here in the past tense. The five preceding elements of the mystery of godliness are accomplished facts and therefore properly presented in the past tense. This one, though future, is so sure of being accomplished that it is presented in the past tense as though it were an accomplished fact already. The same figure of speech is used also in Romans 8:28-30 where the final act in the process (that of being "glorified") is set in the past tense though the last step (being glorified) is future for the believer.

The Fellowship factor in the life of children can not be overstated. The fellowship that children need is that which is centered on the truth of the Word of God rightly divided. It is a fact of life in today's world that local churches that stand for the truth of the Word Rightly divided are small churches. Be that as it may, it is a mistake for parents to attend a church which does not stand for or proclaim the distinctive ministry of Paul to the church the Body of Christ just for their children to have more friends and to be a part of a larger body. As is so often the case when the children convince the parents to go to a larger church that does not stand for dispensational truth, the parents are compromising the truth and are in fact teaching their children that truth is not all that important. Here again the parental example comes into play. Parents who will take a stand for truth and teach their children why truth is important will be instilling in their children spiritual strength and fortitude. Not only that but they will be gaining for themselves and for their children rewards that they will enjoy not only now in this life but also in heaven to come. To make the case we list several key Pauline passages on the subject of rewards for standing for the truth and loss of rewards for failing to do so:

> Reason 1. In 1 Corinthians 3:10-17 "[10] According to the grace of God which is given unto me, as a wise masterbuilder, I have laid the foundation, and another buildeth thereon. But let every man take heed how he buildeth thereupon. [11] For other foundation can no man lay than that is laid, which is Jesus Christ. [12] Now if any man build upon this foundation gold, silver, precious stones, wood, hay, stubble; [13] Every man›s work shall be made manifest: for the day shall declare it, because it shall be revealed by fire; and the fire shall try every man›s work of what sort it is. [14] If any man›s work abide which he hath built thereupon, he shall receive a reward. [15] If any man›s work shall be burned, he shall suffer loss: but he himself shall be saved; yet so as by fire. [16] Know ye not that ye are the temple of God, and *that* the Spirit of God dwelleth in you? [17] If any man defile the temple of God, him shall God destroy; for the temple of God is holy, which *temple* ye are."

In this amazing passage, Paul the apostle describes himself as an architect (master builder) who was given the task of revealing to the world the plans for the church the Body of Christ. The day that Verse 13 speaks about is the day when each believer (parent or child) stands before the judgment seat of Christ. Verse `14 talks about everyman's work being evaluated. The work in question here is the doctrine that the believer stood for and supported. The foundation that Verse 11 talks about is the doctrinal foundation for what is called "the temple of God" in Verse 16. That temple is the place where God lives in the world today – the church the Body of Christ. (Eph. 2:22) The gold, silver and precious stones of Verse 12 are the Pauline doctrine which believers have incorporated into their lives. The non-pauline doctrine is the wood, hay and stubble that will be burned up there at the judgment seat of Christ. How important it is for parents to take a stand for truth and to press upon their children to do the same. Their enjoyment of eternity will be greatly enhanced if they do.

Another passage worthy of consideration in this respect is 2 Timothy 2:8-16. It is a lengthy passage but rich with encouragement to believers who are interested in honoring God with their stand for truth.

> Reason 2. In 2 Timothy 2:8-16 (KJV) [8] Remember that Jesus Christ of the seed of David was raised from the dead according to my gospel: [9] Wherein I suffer trouble, as an evil doer, *even* unto bonds; but the word of God is not bound. [10] Therefore I endure all things for the elect›s sakes, that they may also obtain the salvation which is in Christ Jesus with eternal glory. [11] *It is* a faithful saying: For if we be dead with *him*, we shall also live with *him*: [12] If we suffer, we shall also reign with *him*: if

we deny *him*, he also will deny us: [13] If we believe not, *yet* he abideth faithful: he cannot deny himself. [14] Of these things put *them* in remembrance, charging *them* before the Lord that they strive not about words to no profit, *but* to the subverting of the hearers. [15] Study to shew thyself approved unto God, a workman that needeth not to be ashamed, rightly dividing the word of truth. [16] But shun profane *and* vain babblings: for they will increase unto more ungodliness.

In Verse 10 the apostle speaks of enduring all things (the sufferings of Verse 9) for the elect's sake (that would be you and I who live in this Dispensation of Grace) so that we can obtain the salvation that we have in Christ "<u>with eternal glory</u>." This is soul salvation plus eternal glory. The eternal glory that he is speaking of is in Verse 12 – the glory of reigning with Christ. That goes to those who "suffer" in Verse 12. The word "suffer" is the same word translated "endure" in Verse 10. This is suffering that comes with enduring sound doctrine – the doctrine that Jesus Christ revealed through Paul. This is the same doctrinal foundation that he spoke of in 1Corinthians 3:10 – 12. The suffering is the enduring to stand with those small fellowships which stand for the truth of the word of God rightly divided as he encourages his readers to do in Verse 15. It takes parents who are committed to truth and love for the truth to share that love with their children such that the children gladly stand together with mom and dad to have more to look forward to in glory.

The church entertainment and music: Speaking of the local church, it is important to note that the local church is to be the the pillar and ground of the truth. That means that the local church must be primarily a gospel preaching source of sound Bible doctrine. The sad fact is though that many evangelical churches today are more a source of entertainment than Bible exposition. Also, the entertainment that is presented in many of the largest evangelical churches is an adaptation of the music of the world – rock music. As we consider the three part makeup of man, we note that there is music that appeals to the soul of man, and there is music that appeals to the flesh. There is also music that pleases God, appeals to the spirit, and edifies the soul. The main issue in selection of music should not be what type of music people like, but what type of music suits the purpose that is pursued by a particular gathering. We find eight components of such music which pleases God and edifies the soul and spirit listed in 1Chronicals 16:7-12

1. It gives thanks to the Lord

2. It makes known His deeds.

3. It is singing unto Him

4. It tells of His works

5. It gives glory to His name

6. It expresses the joy of your heart.

7. It brings into memory His wonders and judgements

8. It shows His salvation to all the earth.

J. Vernon McGee made the point well with respect to rock music in the church saying that the "Word of God is being drowned out by the fast beat of rock music emanating from the choir." The syncopation of the rock beat has an innate ability to bring out a basic sensual response from the body. It is purposely aimed at the physical and sensual makeup of man.

The material presented in the pages that follow below has been gleaned from a study entitled "Christian Rock – A Strategem of Mephistopheles" done some time ago by David Nobel who was at the time director of Summit Ministries. David was a former grace pastor but is now home with the Lord. The full article is available from Summit Ministries; P.O. Box 207; Dept. M Manitou Springs, CO 80829.

The Case against Christian Rock

1. The best of rock music appeals to the flesh.

   - There is music that appeals to the soul. Soul music is the music which works on our emotions. Examples might be folk music, soul music, easy listening, classical, etc.

   - There is music which appeals to our spirit. Such is what Paul the apostle spoke of "...speaking to yourselves in psalms and hymns, and spiritual songs, singing with melody in your hearts to the Lord." This type of music works on the intellect and reflects on the riches of God's grace which flows to the believer.

   - There is music which appeals to our flesh. Such music works on our body and tunes into our body's sense of rhythm. Listening to such music tends to captivate our attention through our physical body. Our body "steps to the beat" of such music. Such is rock music.

Man's physical being is essentially rhythmic. There is a rhythm in his respiration, his heart beat, his pulse, his speech, his gait, even is his cerebral hemisphere of his brain. Music tunes into this rhythm and can have a profound effect on man.

2. Rock music originated with Rock Musicians. Rock music is what Rock Stars produce. The life style of rock stars is anything and everything but godly. The heart attitude that produced their life style is communicated in their music. It is an attitude of rebellion against traditional standards and norms. It is truly the music of the world. Like the Pied Piper of Hamlin, the originators of rock music lead young people down a road away from the traditional values of home, family, work, responsibility, and general morality to the valueless and amoral existence of the modern secular man. John Lennon's famous song "Imagine" serves as an illustration:

Imagine there's no heaven.

It's easy if you try

No hell below us

Above us only sky

> Living for today
>
> Imagine there's no countries
>
> It isn't hard to do
>
> Nothing to kill or die for
>
> And no religion too
>
> Imagine all the people
>
> Living life in peace
>
> Imagine no possessions
>
> I wonder if you can
>
> No need for greed or hunger
>
> A brotherhood of man
>
> Imagine all the people
>
> Sharing all the world
>
> You may say I'm a dreamer
>
> But I'm not the only one
>
> I hope some day you join us
>
> And the world will be as one

This piece of music was written in the late 1960's. Anyone familiar with the globalist agenda of groups such as the World Economic Forum today can recognize the global thrust of the world being as one (that was Babel – remember) and the "you will own nothing and be happy" claims of the modern day world elites.

3. Rock music has trademark characteristics that affect the body:

> It has a constant repetition of high pitches
>
> It has very little melody except for often repeated fragments
>
> It has constant repetition of the same chords
>
> It has a breaking up of rhythms
>
> It has unnatural accents
>
> It has constant driving beat that evokes sensual gyrations in the hearers.

While the beat works on the body, it tends to shut down the cognitive (thinking) processes – leaving the mind open to receive the message conveyed in the lyrics. Christian rock groups taking note of this, see rock music as a means of communication of the gospel. But is this a proper mode of propagating the gospel? No! The gospel must be received as a conscious mental decision. Repentance is a change of mind. This requires careful and deliberate thought whereby the facts (facts such as "I am a sinner, God must reject and punish sin, Jesus Christ died for my sins, and that God offers me eternal life as a gift of His grace) are carefully weighted and accepted. The entire Christian life is one of mental reflection as Paul says in Philippians 4:8 "Finally, brethren, whatsoever things are true, whatsoever things *are* honest, whatsoever things *are* just, whatsoever things *are* pure, whatsoever things *are* lovely, whatsoever things *are* of good report; if *there be* any virtue, and if *there be* any praise, think on these things."

There are good reasons for rejecting Christian Rock

1. True Christian worship accents the Spirit. Rock music is sensual in nature. Christian music should give glory to God and edify the believer.

2. Rock music at its outset was of the world, the flesh, and the devil. Why use such music in Christian service?

3. Christian rock is simply welding Christian words to beat music.

4. Christian rock is a compromise with the world.

5. Rock style music sets such strong accent on the rhythm and beat that the words are seldom heard. Christian young people justify listening to secular rock saying they don't listen to the lyrics. On that basis, the argument that Christian rock reaches unbelievers with the gospel is baseless as well.

6. Rock music used in Christian worship conditions Christian young people to listen to secular rock with its content of promiscuity, drugs, violence, and rebellion. This begins the drift toward theological and moral liberalism.

7. Christian rock is a powerful tool in breaking down the barrier which keeps the world out of the church. The church is to be the pillar and ground of the truth (1 Tim. 3:15).

8. Rock music used in church services is divisive. Older saints can not take the loud and heavy rock beat. Good Christian music will appeal to old and young alike. It is contrary to unity of the Spirit (Eph. 4:3-6) to separate the generations. Secular rock music is specifically designed to broaden the generation gap. Paul Kantner of the Jefferson Airplane rock group said "Our music is intended to broaden the generation gap, to alienate children from their parents, and to prepare people for the revolution." Christian young people under the leading and influence of the Word of God are lead to love their parents and to respect their elders.

9. Paul tells Timothy to "lay hands suddenly on no man" (1 Timothy 5:22). Often newly converted drug addicts are made instant leaders without first instructing them on the separated life of the Christian. It is not uncommon to see "drug Freaks" become "Jesus Freaks" by simply substituting Jesus for drugs while continuing their same basic lifestyle."

10. There is much baggage that accompanies rock music (Christian rock included) that the believer is admonished to avoid:

Drug usage (Gal. 5:20)

Filthy language (Eph. 4:29)

Liberal Theology (1 Timothy 4:1)

A worldly lifestyle (1 Thess. 5:21 &22)

People saved out of worldly lifestyles ought to be encouraged to demonstrate their conversion to Christ by doing what the new converts at Ephesus did "Many of them also which used curious arts brought their books together, and burned them before all men..." (Acts 19:19) The result would then be as in Acts 19:20 "So mightily grew the word of God and prevailed."

APPENDIX 1:
THE CHARACTERISTICS OF A MATURE SAINT

A Mature Saint bears the fruit of the Spirit (Gal. 5:22-23) and is therefore:

Forgiving	Eph. 4:32; Col. 3:13
Honest	Eph. 4:25
Vigilant	1Tim. 3:2
Thoughtful	1Cor. 11:33
Patient	Rom. 15:5
Peaceable	Rom. 16:1-16
Gentle	2Tim. 2:2, 4
Faithful	Col. 3:16-24
Modest	1Tim. 2:9
Trusting	1Cor. 13:4-7
Accepting (of self and others)	Rom. 14:13; 15:7
Fair	1Tim. 5:21
Loving	Rom. 13:8; 1Th 3:12; 4:9
Good	Gal. 6:10
Kind	Rom. 12:10
Helpful	Gal. 6:2
Caring	Rom. 15:14; 1Cor 12:25
Empathetic	Rom. 12:15; 15:15; 1Th 4:18
Humble	1Cor. 4:6; Rom. 12:16
Serving	Gal 5:13; Eph 5:21

Self Confident (but not self sufficient – our sufficiency is of God)   2Cor. 3:5

Decisive (but with discernment – he that is spiritual judgeth all things) 1Cor. 6:2-5; 11:31; 2:14-15

What We Do Not Want to See in Our Children

The Works of the Flesh (Gal. 5:19-21) are Manifested as Obnoxious Behavior

> A Demanding Presence
>
> Cruelty
>
> Violent Conduct
>
> Overbearing Demeanor
>
> A Negative Attitude
>
> Self Deprecation
>
> A Critical Spirit
>
> Anger and Bitterness
>
> A Cutting and Caustic Tongue

If we as parents, see these characteristics in our children we must first stop and look as ourselves and our parenting.

We want to see: Builders and not destroyers / Edifiers and not under-miners.

We offer this thought regarding the question: "Is it possible to raise godly children and be fairly sure of the outcome?"

The basic principle behind the requirements of an elder as delineated in 1 Timothy 3:4-5 is "Can this man produce mature saints?" We conclude therefore, that it is possible to raise children to be mature saints. It is truly a shaping and molding process. It is the process that the apostle defines as bringing them up in the nurture and admonition of the Lord (Eph. 6:4)

APPENDIX 2:
OUR HUMAN MAKEUP

1Corinthians 6:19-20 gives us insight into our human makeup and the function of the soul of man. Note the grammar of this verse: "[19] What? know ye not that your body is the temple of the Holy Ghost, *which is* in you, which ye have of God, and ye are not your own? [20] For ye are bought with a price: therefore, glorify God in your body, and in your spirit, which are God>s." Being that this is a direct command, we understand from grammar that the subject is "You." It is the soul that is the "you" that the verse is addressing. We therefore understand that you are a soul who has a body and who also has a spirit and you (the soul that is you) decides what you will do with each.

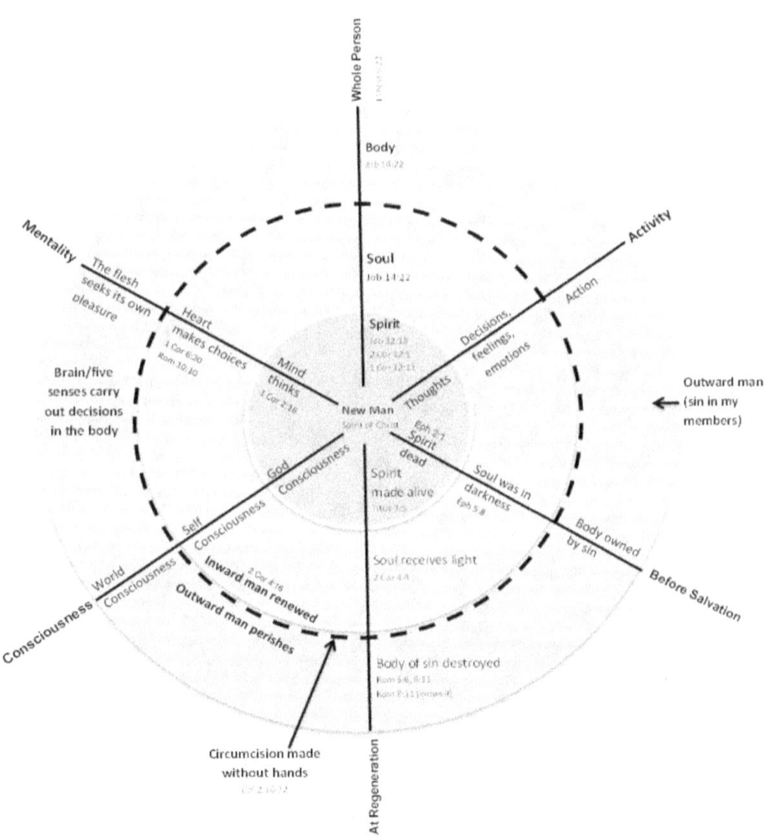

Job 14:22 says of mortal man: "[22] But his flesh upon him shall have pain, and his soul within him shall mourn." God designed the soul to reside within the physical body. The soul is "at home in the Body" as long as our mortal lives persist (2Cor. 5:6).

Elihu's words in Job 32:8 give us understanding of the function of the human spirit: "[8] But *there is* a spirit in man: and the inspiration of the Almighty giveth them understanding." Elihu continues "[18] For I am full of matter, the spirit within me constraineth me." (Job 32:18) It is the spirit in man that provides spiritual constraint to the emotions that reside in the soul. Romans 8:16 gives us insight as to the inter-relationship of the human spirit with the Holy Spirit of God. [16] The Spirit itself beareth witness with our spirit, that we are the children of God: [17] And if children, then heirs; heirs of God, and joint heirs with Christ; if so be that we suffer with *him*, that we may be also glorified together. (Romans 8:16-17)

APPENDIX 3:
NARCISSISM – IS IT SIN OR SICKNESS?

In Chapter 5 we did a study on the perilous times that will befall society in the last days of the Dispensation of Grace. In that chapter, in the section entitled "An Expose of 2Timothy Chapter 3 on the Last Days," we looked at what scripture said about these days – the times in which we live today. In that study of the Bible text we read: "This know also, that in the last days perilous times shall come. For men shall be…" and then the text describes the characteristics of mankind in that time. As we read the characteristics itemized in Verses 2 through 5 of that chapter, we see the personality traits that, in modern parlance, is commonly called "narcissism." I purposely did not use the term "narcissism" there in discussing these character traits in Chapter 5. This author holds the same opinion as was expressed by Jay Adams in his book *Competent to Counsel*. There, in his treatment of such conditions, Adams takes the view that if you tell someone with personality issues that their problem is they are sick, you do two things. Firstly, you give him an excuse to continue with a debilitating character trait because, after all, they are sick and can't help themselves. Secondly, you remove their hope of recovery. If you call it what it is by calling it sin, you can point people to the cure. Sin does have a cure. The cross of Calvary provides the cure for sin. That was the subject and general theme that we explored in Chapter 4 (Grace and the Inner Man) of this book *The Spirit Filled Home* where I did an expose' on our human make up.

Having counseled people in marriage issues, interpersonal relationships, and life experiences in the business world, I have what I believe is a fair grasp of what is the condition called narcissism. As one gets to know the parties involved in narcissistic relationships and the childhood background of each, it is apparent that the condition did not develop in a vacuum. Nature (temperament), nurture, as well as the interpersonal relationships of family and associates during the developmental years of childhood was contributing factors in the development of the condition. That is not to explain away the personal responsibility factor; because, after all, we make our own decisions in life. Therefore, what might be lacking in a healthy personality development due to nature and nurture can be corrected by scripture and one's own response to the spiritual resources that God makes available to us – but more on that later.

What is this condition called Narcissism?

I list here some of the character traits of what people identify as narcissistic personality disorder (NPD). The list below was gleaned from a larger list by Dr. Les Carter in his web site Surviving Narcissism. I list them only for the purpose of comparing them with those characteristics itemized in 2Timothy 3:2-5. We will refer to them collectively as narcissism but I use that term here only for discussion purposes. I prefer to refer to it as the flesh and carnality because that is in fact what it is. Those NPD traits commonly listed by Psychologists are:

1. Grandiosity – an exaggerated sense of self-importance and personal superiority.

2. Self-centeredness – preoccupation with one self, one's accomplishments, and one's problems.

3. Lack of empathy – difficulty understanding and relating to the feelings and needs of others.

4. A strong need for admiration – craving attention, praise, and admiration from others.

5. A sense of entitlement – expecting special treatment and automatic compliance with one's expectation.

6. Exploitive behavior – taking advantage of others to achieve one's own ends with a compulsion to be in control.

7. Envy – resenting the success and accomplishments of others.

8. Arrogance – displaying haughtiness and an air of superiority.

9. Lack of self-awareness – difficulty recognizing one's own failures and weaknesses.

10. Emotional reactivity – overreacting to criticism or perceived slights.

This or similar lists of traits of what people call narcissism can be found in countless web sites, blogs, and You Tube channels on the subject. Until about fifteen or twenty years ago, it seems hardly anyone had heard of such a condition or at least the term was not in common use. As you go through these blogs on NPD, you find that the owners of the web sites commonly will present the situation that there is no cure for this condition. It is taken as an accepted fact that such people will not change. Being that we have listed the common traits of the perceived condition, let's list the common ways that are suggested whereby people can protect themselves from it (i.e. from abuse by narcissists). These are enumerated here not as this author's recommendation but are presented for the rhetorical purpose of furthering a healthy discussion of the theme of Chapter 5 "Dealing with Life in the Twenty-First Century."

As noted above, we use the terms "narcissist" and "narcissism" here only for discussion purposes. It is more constructive for a healthy treatment of the subject to call it what it actually is. It should properly be called sin and it be regarded as a manifestation of what the Bible calls "the flesh."

Commonly proposed recommendations for protecting oneself from the supposed narcissist include:

1. Realize that they are "as is" and that they will not change.

2. Don't take anything personally – the narcissist is just doing what comes naturally to him.

3. Protect your self by establishing boundaries.

4. Believe behavior and not words because narcissists manipulate people with words.

5. Validate your own needs. Do not look to the narcissist to validate your feelings.

I list these proposed recommendations not because I entirely agree with them but because they are offered as recommendations by the blogs and web pages dealing with the subject. I particularly disagree with the first two on this list for reasons stated below. The last three do have merit for people in relationships with and work with people with these traits.

What is troubling about the commonly proposed means of protecting oneself from narcissism is often suggested to be separation or going "no contact." This is troubling because it destroys the very pillar of what makes a family function. There is a Bible based, spiritual alternative to this extreme solution to the problem. The solution to the problem is found in what the Bible calls "walking after the spirit" as in Galatians 5:16 and Romans 8:4. The reader is encouraged to review (reread) Chapter 4 of this book on the subject of walking after the Spirit. God has provided to us who live in the Dispensation of Grace the riches of His grace embodied in the spiritual resources available to us by a faith application of the doctrine of Romans Chapter 6 whereby a Bible believer (a justified person) can have victory over the indwelling sin nature.

The five basic recommendations listed above are actions that would be taken (or advised to be taken) by the target of the narcissistic abuse – the victim. To correct the stressful situation however takes action on the part of the abuser – the narcissist (the victimizer). That, however, is where the difficulty comes in. One of the traits of a so called narcissist is that they tend to shun true introspection. The work of the Holy Spirit of God in baptizing each believer into the death, burial, and resurrection of Christ (Romans 6:1-4) provides us each with a special spiritual resource that gives us victory over the indwelling sin nature. However, to tap into that spiritual resource, one must recognize that the indwelling sin nature is real and that it is indeed the problem. In other words, the so-called "narcissist," if he or she is a believer and is sensitive to the Word of God on the matter, has to own the problem to solve the problem. It is a matter of having an accurate understanding of reality and also of being honest with ourselves and with God.

On this matter of introspection, I offer for consideration the apostle's instruction in 1Corinthians 11:31-32. This passage is in the context of what Paul calls the Lord's Supper. The apostle is taking the Corinthians to task for their unloving conduct and carnal attitudes towards each other in the fellowship. He tells them: "[31] For if we would judge ourselves, we should not be judged. [32] But when we are judged, we are chastened of the Lord, that we should not be condemned with the world." The judging of ourselves in Verse 31 is done based on the Word of God.

In 1Corinthians 3:3-4 he was calling the Corinthians out on their carnality. Note his words to them "[3] For ye are yet carnal: for whereas *there is* among you envying, and strife, and divisions, are ye not carnal, and walk as men? [4] For while one saith, I am of Paul; and another, I *am* of Apollos; are ye not carnal?"

Here in 1Corinthians 11:31 the apostle says, "For if we would judge ourselves, we should not be judged." Who is to do the judging in this passage? It is the believer who would look at his own life and judge what he or she sees based on the Word of God. Is his or her life manifesting the fruit of the Spirit of love, joy, peace, longsuffering, gentleness, goodness, faith, meekness, and temperance (Gal. 5:22-23) or is it the works of the flesh such as hatred, variance, emulations, wrath, strife, seditions, envyings, drunkenness, etc. (Gal. 5:19-21) that are evident? It is the individual believer who is to judge himself but others are judging us in the second part of the verse. This judging is done by others who observe us and assess our character based on what they see and observe. They are living with our fleshly attitude daily. Also in view is the judgment seat of Christ (2Cor. 5:9 & 10) where it will be Christ who will be judging our conduct of life (at least for believers). In either case, the judgment is be based on the Word of God. Then, in Verse 32, he tells us that when we are judged (judged by ourselves based on the Word of God) we are chastened of the Lord.

The Word of God does the judging and it also then does the chastening as we bring our lives into conformance to the Word. The chastening is based on the Word of God working on our regenerated spirits to convict us of changes that we see being needed as a result of our introspection.

If the believers judge themselves and thereby bring their lives in line with the revealed will of God as it is revealed in the Word of God, they will not be judged by others watching and enduring their fleshly walk nor would they suffer loss at the Judgment Seat of Christ. It must be remembered that the "temple of God" in 1Corinthians 3:17 is the Body of Christ – where God lives in the world today. There Paul says "If any man defile the temple of God [by building false doctrine into it] him shall God destroy [i.e. he shall suffer loss at that judgment seat of Christ]; for the temple of God is holy, which temple you are."

In Verse 32 we read: "...we are chastened of the Lord..." Some questions come to mind here regarding this chastening "What is the chastening?" and "What form does that take?" Is there chastening in God's program for the church the Body of Christ in this Dispensation of Grace? Obviously there is for the apostle says so. The apostle indicated in 2Corinthians 6:9 that he was chastened saying "...as chastened but not killed." This chastening would certainly not involve the sleep of death. The words "when we are judged" (1Cor. 11:32) are in the present passive participle. This is therefore not the judgment of self but a judgment that others and the Word of God are doing of us and our conduct. Also, being in the present tense, this is judgment that is going on now in this life. The chastening in Verse 32 is associated with this judgment of self. The word translated "chastened" here is also translated "teaching us" in Titus 2:12. It is also translated "instructing" in 2Timothy 2:2. In both cases, it is the work of God in the believer working through the Word of God that does the work of chastening. We conclude that the same is the case here.

None other than the apostle Paul himself looks at his own life and identifies the problem in Romans Chapter 7 when he placed himself (at least temporarily) under a law whereby he demanded that his flesh perform up to the standards of the Law. In the verses below he shares with us the results:

> "16 If then I do that which I would not, I consent unto the law that *it is* good. 17 Now then it is no more I that do it, but sin that dwelleth in me. 18 For I know that in me (that is, in my flesh,) dwelleth no good thing: for to will is present with me; but *how* to perform that which is good I find not. 19 For the good that I would I do not: but the evil which I would not, that I do. 20 Now if I do that I would not, it is no more I that do it, but sin that dwelleth in me." 21 I find then a law, that, when I would do good, evil is present with me." (Romans 7:16-21)

Note from Verses 17 and 20 of Romans 7 "Now if I do that I would not, it is no more I that do it, but sin that dwelleth in me." That is not a cop out but a statement of fact. The fact is that every believer has a sin nature that he was born with. We find in scripture that our baptism into Christ's death, burial, and resurrection broke sin's power over us (Romans 6:1-4) and placed the Spirit of Christ in our human spirit (Romans 8:11). Chapters 6 through 8 of Romans go into great detail in describing what it is in man (including in believers) that causes our interpersonal problems and conflicts. We made note in Table 2 (in Chapter 3) that there are three basic sources for what it is that forms our character – those being nature, nurture, and, of course, scripture. Nature is of course what we were born with. This would include things such as our temperament and a sin nature. There is nothing that we can do with that except to realize that it is what it is. Nurture is what we lived with growing up. That is the home life that we grew up under and other of life's expeeeriences. There is little that we can do about that either. However, there is much that we can do with the scripture. Scripture teaches us how the Holy Spirit of God works in the believer to effect positive change. The most fundamental point of doctrine on the impact of Scripture on character development is probably in 1Corinthians 2:14-16

> "[14] But the natural man receiveth not the things of the Spirit of God: for they are foolishness unto him: neither can he know *them*, because they are spiritually discerned. [15] But he that is spiritual judgeth all things, yet he himself is judged of no man. [16] For who hath known the mind of the Lord, that he may instruct him? But we have the mind of Christ."

The natural man in this text is the unsaved man to whom the things of the Spirit of God are foolishness. "He that is spiritual…" however, is a man who has trusted Christ as Savior and has gotten into the Word of God (rightly divided) and has therefore formed in his human spirit the mind of Christ. Before going into the spiritual resource for deliverance from the power of sin, we should look at some of the childhood origins of what causes the spiritual condition that is called narcissism.

The childhood origin of narcissism

I direct the reader's attention to Chapter 7 of this book and especially to Table 4 in that chapter. In that table we listed three categories of discipline. Those being: Too Harsh of discipline, Loving Discipline, and No Discipline. It is this author's opinion that either of the two extremes (too severe of discipline, unloving discipline, or no discipline) can lead to (but are not the sole source of) the narcissistic traits listed above.

Too harsh discipline, especially when it is not done in love, can be received and perceived by the child as being done out of contempt for the personhood of the child including an element of rejection on the part of the parent. The carnal mind set is then simply the response of the sin nature in the child responding to what he or she perceives as mistreatment and abuse. The condition then is basically a defense mechanism in which the child's own sin nature works together with what is an instinct for survival.

Children have an innate sense of right on wrong. Children have a need to be loved, cherished, and valued and to be recognized as a person whose fellowship is of great value to their parents. In a healthy parent – child relationship, the validity of the child as a precious partner in life is self-evident to both. If what children perceive that they are getting from those who should be their source of supply of love, protection, validity as a real person of value, and unconditional acceptance is instead a disdain or (heaven forbid) even contempt, the child is truly traumatized in his very soul. The child then, acting with a natural fleshly response, develops coping mechanisms whereby the child creates a false and imaginary persona whereby he sees himself having achieved that which would have brought for him the admiration he craves. This complex relationship of the indwelling sin nature and the developing coping mechanism leads to some characteristics that tend toward a toxic personality profile. I list some of these coping mechanisms here:

- The development of a manipulative and exploitive nature to gain the affirmation he is now missing and which he craves.

- The child is compelled to somehow gain control over people around them at all costs to protect himself. He begins to cultivate the art of controlling people by manipulation.

- The child, sensing that somehow his true self is not adequate to gain approval, develops a false persona which he lives out and which he seeks to protect from discovery.

- The child develops a certain charm and charisma that enables him to function in social settings without letting his true self be known. The child in adulthood then becomes adept at hiding the condition.

- Envy of those who he sees receiving the affirmation he desires becomes a constant companion with him.

- Development of extreme sensitivity to criticism whereby he feels compelled to reject such negative assessment of his conduct and to lash out in anger at those who would dare to criticize him.

- He becomes an over achiever in his attempt to gain the attention, affection, praise, and admiration that he seeks while yet harboring the thought that he cannot be good enough to gain it.

- Perhaps the most destructive part of this condition is the lack of empathy. He did not see empathy modeled in those who he looked to in order to be loved and be accepted and so did not develop that part of his interpersonal skills set. After all, when he looked for love and found disdain, he concludes it must be that concern for the feelings of others is not a natural part of a normal healthy life.

No discipline can also lead to certain narcissistic traits. To take the approach in discipline that "My child can do no wrong" and thus ignore discipline and the loving application of chastisement would be the making of a prima donna (or of its male counterpart). The child who grows up as a prince or princess while never having been disciplined for self-centered conduct grows up with a sense of entitlement. The characteristics of such unchecked conduct include:

- The child grows up with a sense of superiority whereby he believes all others are beneath him.

- A lack of empathy for the feelings and needs of others.

- A sense of entitlement whereby the child believes that "I am special and deserving of special treatment."

- The child develops an arrogant and haughty attitude.

At this point in our study, it should be noted that there is probably a certain number of narcissistic traits in everyone who has a sin nature. That would cover everyone but our Lord Himself. Good parenting, however, addresses those traits as they show up in the personality we see in our children. Preteens are just developing empathy for others and have not developed enough of their persona to manipulate people yet. Teens are typically still somewhat self-centered, and we do not see enough of the classic traits of a fleshly walk to call it narcissism. It is not until young people get into their mid-twenties that what is called NPD really starts to show up. There are however, things that parents should watch for in their teens. The following are some red flag markers to take note of:

- Persistent bullying behavior such as making fun of others, threatening others, and degrading others.

- Persistent need to win no matter what or who might get hurt.

- Persistent lying to benefit oneself.

- Egotistical view of extraordinary self-worth.

- Preoccupation with getting one's own needs met with disregard to the needs of others.

- Entitled attitude – acting as if they deserve special treatment.

- Aggressive response to being criticized.

- Blaming others for a bad outcome.

- Being much more competitive than cooperative.

The question then is: once parents see these red flags, how should these attitudes be addressed? The following teaching techniques (teaching tools) should be in the parenting tool chest:

- Call the preteen out on this ungodly behavior.

- Teach empathy. By the time children get into their teen years, they should be able to sympathize with others and begin to feel their pain.

- Value character traits like honesty and kindness over being tough and dominant.

- Change entitled attitudes and stop entitled actions.

- Squelch greed. Promote sharing.

- Insist that they treat others as they desire to be treated. This is a hard one to teach but don't give up.

- Build a healthy self-image (Eph. 1:4). This includes children seeing themselves as sinners saved by grace but made accepted by God the Father because they are in Christ.

- Don't allow blaming others for one's own problems and failures. Encourage them to admit to their failures and work through them.

- Teach Critical Thinking Skills:

  Teach how to discern between truths and falsehood.

  Teach how to recognize manipulation when it is encountered.

Discipline must always be done in love. Love, respect, and deeply held desire for the temporal and eternal welfare of the child must be first and foremost in the mind and heart of the parent in discipline. Discipline must be rooted in the premise that is ever present in a parent's thought and consciousness that says, "I love you too much to let you get by with such inappropriate conduct that will limit your full development as a child of God."

The solution to the problem – the true cure for narcissism is found in Chapter 6 of Romans. We covered this in Chapter Four of this study but we present a brief summary here.

"[5] For if we have been planted together in the likeness of his death, we shall be also *in the likeness* of *his* resurrection: [6] Knowing this, that our old man is crucified with *him*, that the body of sin[g] might be destroyed, that henceforth we should not serve sin." (Romans 6:5–6)

"[11] Likewise **reckon** ye also yourselves to be dead indeed unto sin, but alive unto God through Jesus Christ our Lord. [12] Let **not sin therefore reign** in your mortal body, that ye should obey it in the lusts thereof. [13] Neither **yield** ye your members *as* instruments of unrighteousness unto sin: but **yield** yourselves unto God, as those that are alive from the dead, and your members *as* instruments of righteousness unto God. [14] For sin shall not have dominion over you: for ye are not under the law, but under grace." (Romans 6:11–14)

The doctrine of deliverance from the power, reign, and dominion of sin (the old Adamic sin nature) is given in Romans 6:1–6. The means by which it is appropriated is in Verses 8-14. There are three actions needed to appropriate the victory of that deliverance:

1. Believe that our baptism into Christ's death delivers us from both the penalty of sin and also from the power of sin and made us alive unto God. (Verses 8-10)

2. Reckon it to be a fact that we are indeed dead unto sin but alive unto God through Christ. (Verses 11-12)

3. Refuse to yield the use of the members our bodies to the old sin nature (i.e. to old Mr. Sin) but rather yield ourselves unto God as those who are alive from the dead to yield our members as instruments of righteousness unto God (Verses 13–14). This is a moment by moment, occasion by occasion decision that we make as believers to appropriate victory over sin.

4. Above all, the believer, whether he is the victim or the victimizer, needs to see himself in Christ. The victim needs to find in the love of the Father for him or her as being sufficient to satisfy his need for unconditional love and acceptance because that is what the believer has in Christ. The victimizer then must be honest with himself and recognize that he is allowing sin, a defeated enemy, to run his life and is destroying what can be a rich and rewarding life in Christ.

5. The victim of such "narcissistic abuse," as long as the abuser does not or is not willing to examine himself or herself, needs to establish boundaries in their relationship. There is a book *Boundaries in Marriage* by Cloud and Townsend that comes highly recommended that explains how boundaries can set and used to avoid abuse bt a partner who walks after the flesh.

We urge the reader to review all of Chapter 4 of this book and also Chapter 6 of Romans again. However for a quick reference, I call your attention to the verbs used in this passage.

- The verb **reckon** in Verse 11 of Romans Chapter 6 is in the present tense and middle voice. It is looking back at Verses 6 & 7. Verse 6 tells us that the believer's physical body has had a change of ownership and it no longer belongs to the sin nature that still dwells in it. Therefore, he does not have to allow sin to reign in his mortal body. Sin's right to our physical body has been broken by the baptizing work of Verses 1 through 4.

- The phrase "**Let not sin therefore reign**" in Romans 6:12 is in the present active imperative. It is telling the believer to not be continually allowing the sin nature to rule in his life. This is a decision that the believer must be continually making. The sin nature desires to run the believer's life but the work of the Holy Spirit in baptizing the believer into Christ's death, burial and resurrection (Romans 6:1-4) had broken its power over us.

- The first use of the verb **yield** in 6:13 is also in the present active imperative. It tells the believer to not be continually allowing the sin nature to have the use of the members on your body to do its deeds of the flesh.

- The second use of the verb **yield** in Verse 13 is again in the present active imperative. Only here it is telling the believer to be continually yielding to God as one who now has new life from Him. This is Galatians 2:20-21 in action: "[20] I am crucified with Christ: nevertheless, I live; yet not I, but Christ liveth in me: and the life which I now live in the flesh I live by the faith of the Son of God, who loved me, and gave himself for me. [21] I do not frustrate the grace of God: for if righteousness *come* by the law, then Christ is dead in vain."

Victory over what is commonly called narcissism but should be called carnality is available to the person who is caught up in this fleshly manifestation of the sin nature. However, to appropriate that victory, one must first trust the Lord Jesus Christ as Savior and then he must be ready to admit that it is sin that dwells in him in his flesh (Rom. 7:18) that causes the problem. By the believer in an act of faith applying the doctrine of Romans Chapter 6, he or she can have the victory of being set free from sin as a master. It is truly as Romans 6:14 says "[14]For sin shall not have dominion over you: for ye are not under the law, but under grace." May it be that all believers discover the blessed option to live allowing grace to reign. "[21] That as sin hath reigned unto death, even so might grace reign through righteousness unto eternal life by Jesus Christ our Lord." (Rom. 5:21)

The solution to the problem – the true cure for narcissism is found in Chapter 6 of Romans. We covered this in Chapter four of this study.

> "[5] For if we have been planted together in the likeness of his death, we shall be also *in the likeness* of *his* resurrection: [6]Knowing this, that our old man is crucified with *him*, that the body of sin[g] might be destroyed, that henceforth we should not serve sin." (Romans 6:5–6)

The doctrine of deliverance from the power, reign, and dominion of sin (the old Adamic sin nature) is given in Romans 6:1–6. The means by which it is appropriated is in Verses 7-14. There are three actions needed to appropriate the victory of that deliverance. They are: 1) Trust Jesus Christ as your personal Savior. 2) Recognize that sin will continue to run your life if you allow it to. And 3) Walk after the Spirit by applying the doctrine of grace by faith in the Word of God rightly divided.

In Conclusion: What is commonly called narcissism is not so much a pathological condition as it is a spiritual condition. It is a condition that can be solved by: 1) "rightly dividing the word of truth (2Timothy 2:15) and 2) "walking after the Spirit."

APPENDIX 4:
MARRIAGE, DIVORCE AND REMARRIAGE IN THE DISPENSATION OF GRACE

It was suggested to me by one of the reviewers of this study of the Spirit Filled Home to also include a section on marriage, divorce and remarriage. To that end, this Appendix has been added as a separate treatment of this very pertinent and contemporary subject. It is particularly important because there is a an important dispensational aspect to the subject. To see how the law of marriage changed through time we consider the passage in Matthew Chapter 5 where we find the Lord pressing the Law to the fullest. He tells the Israel at the outset of His earthly ministry "Think not that I am come to destroy the law, or the prophets: I am not come to destroy, but to fulfil." (Matthew 5:17) "Fulfill" meaning to fully fill the Law or to press it to its fullest, strictest interpretation. We see Him do that with the Law of Marriage in Matthew 5:31-32 saying "[31]It hath been said, Whosoever shall put away his wife, let him give her a writing of divorcement: [32] But I say unto you, That whosoever shall put away his wife, saving for the cause of fornication, causeth her to commit adultery: and whosoever shall marry her that is divorced committeth adultery." This strict interpretation of the Law of Moses was in accordance with his earthly ministry to Israel when He is proclaiming the Kingdom of Heaven as being at hand (ready to be set up). Had Israel trusted the Lord Jesus Christ as Messiah, the Kingdom of Heaven would have been set up and the present Dispensation of Grace would not have happened. However, Israel did reject Jesus Christ as Messiah and the offer of the Kingdom of Heaven was withdrawn. With the saving of Saul of Tarsus, God started the Dispensation of Grace and began to preach a new message to the world through him. The new message is called "the preaching of Jesus Christ according to the revelation of the mystery." With that, "...old things are passed away and all things have become new..." (2Cor. 5:17) To learn how marriage has changed in this present Dispensation of Grace, we go to First Corinthians Chapter 7. The following is an expose of that chapter. The chapter can be outlined as being in three sections with each pursuing a theme regarding marriage as follows:

- Theme I: 1Corinthians 7:1-9 says in effect: "It is good for the single man or woman who can remain single and still maintain moral purity to do so" (this applies specifically to any unmarried and, in 1Corinthians 7:24-40, to virgins).

- Theme II: 1Corinthians 7:10-11 says in effect: "Each believer who is married to another believer has a responsibility to stay married to that believer."

- Theme III: 1Corinthians 7:12-24 says in effect: "Each believer who is married to an unbeliever is to faithfully maintain that marriage unless the unbeliever departs."

Theme I

" [1] Now concerning the things whereof ye wrote[a] unto me: *It is* good for a man not to touch[b] a woman. [2] Nevertheless, *to avoid* fornication, let[c] every man have his own wife, and let every woman have her own husband. [3] Let the husband[d] render unto the wife due benevolence: and likewise also the wife unto the husband. [4] The wife hath not power of her own body, but the husband: and likewise also the husband hath not power of his own body, but the wife. [5] Defraud ye not one the other, except *it be* with consent[e] for a time, that ye may give yourselves to fasting and prayer; and come together again, that Satan tempt you not for your incontinency. [6] But I speak this by[f] permission, *and* not of commandment. [7] For I would that all men were even as I myself. But every man hath his proper gift[g] of God, one after this manner, and another after that. [8] I say therefore to the unmarried[h] and widows, It is good for them if they abide even as I. [9] But if they cannot contain, let them[i] marry: for it is better to marry than to burn." (1Corinthians 7:1-9)

Annotated Notes from the Bible Text

[a] To understand the epistle of First Corinthians, we need to understand that it was precipitated by the Corinthians writing a letter to Paul with some questions. Paul is here in Chapter 7 of this epistle, finally getting around to answering the various questions that the Corinthians raised. We don't have the advantage of reading the Corinthians' letter to Paul and see these questions. However, we can figure out what they might have been based on clues given in Paul's answers. It is apparent from Chapter 7 that the first question being addressed was essentially "Is it proper for a man to remain unmarried?"

[b] Paul starts out saying "It is good for a man not to touch (translated in the infinitive, meaning not to know carnally) a woman." This is a simple statement that it is a good thing for a man (although it applies equally to both sexes) to remain celibate. However, to avoid fornication, every man should have his own wife and every woman her own husband. The division of the race between the two sexes is God's provision for the procreation of the race. God created man as a race of free moral agents which can reproduce more free moral agents. Sex, therefore, is of divine origin and is a thing to be enjoyed and appreciated. The attraction between the sexes is a natural phenomenon and can be either used or abused. God ordained that it be expressed and this natural desire be vented only in the context of marriage (cf Heb 4:12).

[c] Paul, the apostle of the Gentiles, is saying that it is imperative for those who cannot maintain self control to get married. Fornication is illicit sex outside of marriage. We must remember that it is "on account of" fornication—on account of the ever-present risk of believers being caught up in this sin, that this imperative is given. Note that Paul does not here impose any limits on who may or may not marry in order to avoid fornication. He simply states that those who are in danger of falling prey to this sin are to marry to avoid it. We ask the question at this point: "Should anyone who is in danger of fornication be denied this safety net?" We ask this question here trusting that the remainder of this chapter will give us an answer to it.

[d] In Verse 3 the apostle tells husband and wives to render unto each other all due benevolence. "Due benevolence" here means that which is properly owed and due; it is a duty. Marriage is an institution of mutual responsibilities

between husband and wife. Men and women are constructed differently to meet each others' physical needs and are wired differently so that we can likewise meet each others' emotional needs. It is our duty to provide to our mates that for which God equipped us to provide. "Render" is in the present imperative, indicating that it is not an option but a requirement that we meet our mate's needs. The wife hath not "power of" (authority over) her own body. In terms of conjugal relationship, the wife is to passively yield her body to her husband and not to withhold it. So too the husband must passively yield his body to his wife so as to meet her needs (physically and emotionally). "But" in Verse 4 is the strong adversative. For a believer to refuse his/her mate of the sexual favors of his/her body would be to "defraud" (to steal or cheat) his/her mate of something that is due them.

[e] The apostle allows the abstinence from sexual relationship if it is for a time and with mutual consent. "With consent" is the word from which we get our word "symphony". Every aspect of the believer's marriage should be as coordinated with one's spouse as a symphony. Abstinence from conjugal relationships should be only "for a time" and then only "with consent" and only for worthy reasons such as fasting and prayer. There is a danger if abstinence is carried on too long. Incontinency here in Verse 5 is referring to a lack of ability to withstand or to control the sex drive.

[f] Lest any believer reading this should think that he/she is being commanded to engage in this type of fasting (i.e. to abstain from conjugal relationships between marriage partners), Paul states clearly that this is given as permission and not as a commandment. The Pauline revelation has the believer under grace and not under law. The next verse starts with the connecting word "for" to relate with Verse 7 with the permission of Verses 5 & 6. Paul enjoyed the gift of celibacy and he wished that all men could enjoy it as well. To be celibate as Paul would be not only to abstain from sexual gratification on a temporary basis (Verse 5) but to do so on a permanent basis.

[g] Being married is a gift but being able to maintain sexual purity in an unmarried state is also. The "Therefore" in Verse 8 is there because of Verse 7. Paul enjoyed the single, celibate state and recommends it to those who can do it and maintain a sanctified life. His words "I would" is not the determinative will, but a wish. He recommends the celibate life but does not in any way insist on it.

[h] The word for "unmarried" is used only five times in the New Testament. All five are in this chapter. In Verse 11, it is used with reference to a separated woman. The word for widows is the word for bereaved. It is important to note, though he distinguishes between the unmarried (whether virgins or separated or reformed fornicators) and widows (bereaved whether man or woman), he does not forbid either from marrying. He is in Verse 8 simply instructing them that their life would be easier if they remained single.

[i] Paul qualifies his recommendation to remain single with this exception: if they cannot maintain self control and are in danger of compromising their sanctification (in terms of sexual purity), they should marry. Marriage is always the safety net that is available to any single person who wants and desires God's will but has trouble maintaining sexual purity. For the one who left his or her marriage partner, this would mean getting back together with his/her mate. We will see more on this later. The words "Let them marry" is in the imperative mode. The one who cannot otherwise maintain self control is to marry. Paul referring to the burning passion that the creator put within men and

women so as to provide for marriage and the family. This passion is a natural part of the human make up and God has provided the proper means for its expression—marriage.

[j] At this point (Verse 10) it would be good to back up and take a look at the chapter as a whole by viewing the brief outline of the themes:

- Theme I: 1Corinthians 7:1-9 -- It is good for the single man or woman who can remain single and still maintain moral purity to do so. (this applies specifically to any unmarried

- and in 1Corinthians 7:24-40 to virgins)

- Theme II: 1Corinthians 7:10-11 -- Each believer who is married to another believer has a responsibility to stay married to that believer.

- Theme III: 1Corinthians 7:12-24 -- Each believer who is married to an unbeliever is to faithfully maintain that marriage unless the unbeliever departs.

Theme II
The case of two believers married to each other

"[10] And unto the married I command, *yet* not I, but[k] the Lord, Let not the wife depart[l] from *her* husband: [11] But and if she depart, let her remain[m] unmarried, or be reconciled[n] to *her* husband: and let not the husband put away[o] *his* wife. [12] But to the rest speak I, not the Lord: If any brother hath a wife that believeth not, and she be pleased to dwell with him, let him not put her away." (1Cor. 7:10-12)

[k] In Verse 10, Paul talks about something that both he and the Lord command while in Verse 12 he speaks about something that he commands but not the Lord. This is not a case of some scripture being "uninspired" or somehow less than the "inerrant Word of God" as some suggest. Rather, Paul speaks as "the apostle of the Gentiles" (Rom 11:13) while our Lord, during His earthly ministry, was "a minister of the circumcision" (Rom 15:8). While our Lord ministered to Israel, He dealt with a covenant people. A Jew could be saved by placing his faith in the covenant that God made with his/her people. Every Jew, however, was under the covenant (until it was interrupted to allow for the Dispensation of the Grace of God). There was to be no one in that nation who was outside of the kingdom of God (though we know that there were some). Paul on the other hand was committed with "the Gospel of the uncircumcision" (Gal. 2:7). Under grace, in God's program among the nations today, it is possible to have someone who is in the kingdom of God being married to someone who is outside of it. Therefore, Paul, under the direction of Christ (1Tim. 6:3 & Gal. 1:12) wrote special instructions on how to deal with that possibility (1Cor. 14:37).

[l] Let not the wife (a believing wife) depart from her husband. The passive voice here implies that there would be others involved who would encourage and/or in some way promote the separation. She is to take no action to separate herself, and no other believer is to take action to promote such a separation. The passive voice speaks of the process of divorce in which other (the state, society, the courts, etc.) become involved. "Depart" speaks again of divorce. The divorced believer is to remain unmarried or be reconciled with his/her believing mate. What we ask is, "Who

enforces this?" Obviously, if a believer is divorcing his or her believing mate to marry another, he/she is in rebellion to God and to the direct command of scripture so that he/she is not going to yield to the Word on this. Though this is a command of God for the departing believer, the instruction is given to the assembly at large and the elders in particular for administration. The issue here is "Who will you allow in fellowship?" The epistle of First Corinthians is actually focused heavily on the corporate life of a local church.

[m] The woman who "is departed" from her husband in Verse 11 is regarded as "unmarried." The Pauline revelation is "the dispensation of the grace of God" (Eph. 3:2). It is not an opportunity for sin or license. Grace does not condone the glorified wife-swapping that the secular world partakes in during this divorce-ridden "present evil age". For the believer, the grass might look greener on the other side of the fence, but his responsibility before God is to abide within the pasture allotted to him. The believer who, in spite of this clear instruction to remain faithful to her spouse, departs (divorces), she has two options: 1. remain in a single state, or 2. be reconciled to her husband. The same applies for the reverse situation of a husband leaving his wife as well. If she rebels against this and marries another man, the assembly must express its disapproval by dis-fellowshipping her. It is the corporate life of the assembly at large that Paul has reference to here. The issue with the Corinthians, as Paul addresses it in this epistle, is how the assembly deals with sin in its midst.

[n] Who is to remain unmarried? We noted and asked the question in Note 4, "Should anyone who is in danger of fornication be denied this safety net?" Let's address the issue a bit here. Let's consider the often-recurring situation of a faithful mate (faithful in the sense of fidelity to the marriage contract) being abandoned by an unfaithful partner. The offending party not only divorced him/her but then went on to marry another. As time goes on, we find that the faithful partner does not have that gift that would allow her/him to live a holy life in a single state. Does that mean that this faithful mate (the abandoned marriage partner who is now "loosed") should not be allowed to remarry? Let's note that the issue is "fellowship in the assembly." To forbid this party who has demonstrated faithfulness the right to remarry would be to put this individual (and the assembly) under law. It is the offending party who is to "remain unmarried" or be reconciled. The faithful party however is to demonstrate faithfulness by being available as long as there is any hope for reconciliation.

[o] It is interesting to note that the unfaithful wife "departs" while the unfaithful husband "puts away" his wife. The word for "put away" is the present active infinitive for the word meaning "to send away." The action of the husband is seen to be active while that of the wife is seen to be passive. This is in keeping with the emotional and spiritual make up of men and women as God made them different. God designed the man to be the initiator and the woman to be the responder (follower)—particularly since the fall in Eden (Gen. 3:16). The husband is to use that God-given leadership to be aggressively benevolent on behalf of his wife (and children). To send her away is to violate this sacred trust.

Note that the injunction for the husband to "not put away his wife" is in the indicative mode and not the imperative mode of command. This would allow for the possible circumstances that potentially could develop. Note also that adultery on the part of the wife is not necessarily grounds for divorcement on the part of the husband (or vice versa). Though this was required under Israel's program (Matt. 5:32; cf. Deut. 22:22), grace encourages forgiveness (Eph. 4:32) where repentance is manifested.

Theme III
The case of a believer married to an unbeliever

> "¹³ And the woman which hath an husband that believeth[p] not, and if he be pleased to dwell[q] with her, let her not leave him. ¹⁴ For the unbelieving husband is sanctified[r] by the wife, and the unbelieving wife is sanctified by the husband: else were your children unclean; but now are they holy. ¹⁵ But if the unbelieving depart, let him depart. A brother or a sister is not under bondage in such *cases*: but God hath called[s] us to peace. ¹⁶ For what knowest thou, O wife, whether thou shalt save *thy* husband? or how knowest thou, O man, whether thou shalt save *thy* wife?" (1Cor. 7:13-16)

[p] Having addressed the issue of believers married to believers and that of the unmarried, Paul talks about the matter of believers being married to unbelievers in Verses 13 thru 16. This situation could come about either as one mate gets saved after marriage or by carelessness as a believer marries an unbeliever. The latter situation is contrary to the will of God (1Cor. 7:39; *cf.* 2Cor 6:14).

[q] Paul does not tell the unbeliever what to do (*cf* 1Cor. 5:12). His instruction is to the believer. However, Paul does respect the unbeliever's will in the matter. Here in Verses 12-13, he instructs the believer to consider whether or not the unbeliever "be pleased to dwell" with him/her. The believer has resources to draw upon that the unbeliever does not—i.e. the indwelling "Spirit of Christ" (Rom. 8:9); the crucifixion of the old man (Rom 6:1-4); spiritual circumcision (Col. 2:10-14); the intercessory work of Christ (Rom. 8:34) and of the Holy Spirit (Rom. 8:26-27); regeneration (Rom. 8:11; Titus 3:5), etc. Therefore, God can and does require the believer to live a victorious life in spite of circumstances. The grace of God will always win over the circumstances of life if we by faith appropriate it (Rom. 8:1-4; 5:20). The discussion of Note 23 will explain the difference between the wording here, for wives and husbands.

[r] The unbelieving mate is sanctified by the believing mate (Verse 14) in that God recognizes and blesses the marriage for the sake of the believer. If it were not so, the children of the believer would be illegitimate. God regards this unbeliever as different from other unbelievers for the sake of the believing mate and the believer's children. It does not mean that the unbeliever is any different with respect to sin and his need of redemption. If the unbelieving mate is not pleased to stay in the marriage and takes action to depart, the believer is not to resist the action. The words "is not under bondage" in Verse 15 is in the perfect passive indicative tense. God definitely and definitively loosed that person and that believer is, as a result, loosed. Being loosed, that person is free to marry again and still be in fellowship (see Note 14).

[s] The words "but God has called us to peace" is key here. Peace, along with grace and mercy, is a hallmark describing the Dispensation of the Grace of God. The believer is to do everything possible to "live peaceably with all men" (Rom. 12:18). As long as an unbeliever in a marriage with a believer can conduct himself in a peaceful/non-abusive manner, it is good that the marriage continue. However, if the situation becomes abusive, it is better to let the unbeliever depart so that there can be peace in the home.

Believers are to do nothing rash regarding their status in coming to Christ for salvation.

"[17] But as God hath distributed to every man, as the Lord hath called[t] every one, so let him walk. And so ordain I in all churches. [18] Is any man called being circumcised? let him not become[u] uncircumcised. Is any called in uncircumcision? let him not be circumcised. [19] Circumcision is nothing, and uncircumcision is nothing, but the keeping of the commandments of God. [20] Let every man abide in the same calling wherein he was called. [21] Art thou called *being* a servant? care not for it: but if thou mayest be made free, use *it* rather. [22] For he that is called in the Lord, *being* a servant, is the Lord's freeman: likewise also he that is called, *being* free, is Christ's servant. [23] Ye are bought with a price; be not ye the servants of men. [24] Brethren, let every man, wherein he is called, therein abide with God." (1Cor. 7:17-23)

[t] Paul seems to be going into a different subject here in Verse 17 but yet he still continues the same idea—i.e. remaining in the same occupational, social, or marital status in which one was called. The term "has distributed to" means "to assign to." It is translated "has dealt to" in Romans 12:3. "God has dealt to every man the measure of faith" in the sense that God has assigned to each an area of occupation in which to be faithful. Coming to Christ for salvation was not to result in the radical casting off of the responsibilities that were in place before salvation. Salvation in the Dispensation of the Grace of God is not a revolutionary movement, but an inward change in the heart. Salvation in the kingdom program for Israel will be a complete change of the status quo. Those who have divorced before salvation are not called to or bound to go back and undo the divorce. Those who married an unbeliever before salvation are not to leave the marriage if the mate is pleased to maintain the marriage.

[u] There is some debate if the reference to being circumcised here is referring to the physical rite or to the dispensational distinction between one who is a member of the circumcision and one who is a member of the uncircumcision. Paul is not referring to the physical rite of circumcision for to become uncircumcised would be impossible. He is referring to those called as a member of the circumcision (Gal. 2:7) verses one who is called under the gospel of the grace of God. The gist of Verses 17 thru 23 is that if you are called being married, do not seek to be unmarried or for that matter don't seek to change your social status except that if you can be free to serve the Lord better, do so.

General Advice to Virgins, the Bound and the Unmarried regarding Marriage

"[25] Now concerning virgins I have no commandment of the Lord: yet I give my judgment, as one that hath obtained mercy of the Lord to be faithful. [26] I suppose therefore that this is good for the present[v] distress, *I say*, that *it is* good for a man so to be. [27] Art thou bound unto a wife? seek not to be loosed. Art thou loosed from a wife? seek not a wife. [28] But and if thou marry, thou hast not sinned; and if a virgin marry, she hath not sinned. Nevertheless such shall have trouble in the flesh: but I spare you. . [29] But this I say, brethren, the time *is* short: it remaineth, that both they that have wives be as though they had none; [30] And they that weep, as though they wept not; and they that rejoice, as though they rejoiced not; and they that buy, as though they possessed not; [31] And they that use this world, as not abusing *it*: for the fashion of this world passeth away. [32] But I would have you without carefulness. He that is unmarried careth for the things that belong to the Lord, how he may please the Lord: [33] But he that is married careth for the things that are of the world, how he may please *his* wife. **³⁴** There is difference *also* between a wife and a virgin. The unmarried woman careth for the things of the Lord, that she may be holy both in body and in spirit: but she that is married careth for the things of the world, how she may please *her* husband. **³⁵** And this I speak for your own profit; not that I may cast a snare upon you, but for that which is comely, and that ye may attend upon the Lord without distraction." (1Cor. 7:25-36)

[v]. Paul is offering advice here in regard to the present distress. When Paul wrote this there was great persecution directed against believers. In light of this, he offers his opinion on the best course of action regarding marriage. This advice:

- If you are bound to a wife, don't seek to be loosed (Verse 27).

- If you are loosed from a wife (either by loss of the wife by death or by her departing in spite of your efforts to stay married), don't seek a wife. (Verse 27)

- If you marry, you have not sinned (Verse 28).

- If a virgin marries, she has not sinned (Verse 28).

- This life will not last long so stay free to serve the Lord if you can (Verses 29 – 33).

- If you marry, do so with the understanding that there are responsibilities that go along with it (Verses 34-36).

    "**³⁶** But if any man think that he behaveth himself uncomely toward his[w] virgin, if she pass the flower of *her* age, and need so require, let him do what he will, he sinneth not: let them marry. **³⁷** Nevertheless he that standeth stedfast in his heart, having no necessity, but hath power over his own will, and hath so decreed in his heart that he will keep his virgin, doeth well. **³⁸** So then he that giveth *her* in marriage doeth well; but he that giveth *her* not in marriage doeth better." (1Cor. 7:36-38)

[w]. In Verses 36 thru 38 the apostle offers advice to fathers whose virgin daughters are still living at his home. In Christian homes, daughters ought to seek the advice of her father regarding who she marries and whether she should marry. The expression here "to keep his virgin" refers to him supporting her financially as long as he can financially do so. The father who gives her in marriage does well but he that does not give her does better. This is a culturally dependent thing. In modern society, not many Christian daughters (unfortunately) will actually forgo marriage because her father does not give his consent.

APPENDIX 5:
RIGHTLY DIVIDING THE WORD OF TRUTH

Half of the New Testament deals with Bible Prophecy, the twelve apostles, and Israel while the other half deals with the Mystery revealed through Paul. The Book of Acts is the transition between the two programs. The Book of Romans presents the atoning blood of Christ in the mystery program while the Book of Hebrews does so for Israel and the Kingdom program. The table on the facing page lays out the differences between the two programs

This page contains an illustration of the books of the New Testament stacked according to the program to which they pertain. Paul as the apostle of the Gentiles reveals to the world the mystery concerning the dispensation of the grace of God (Eph. 3:1-4). His writings present to us the preaching of Jesus Christ according to the revelation of the mystery. The Pauline epistles culminate with the rapture of the church, the Body of Christ to Heaven – its eternal home (2Cor. 5:1). The circumcision epistles present the preaching of Jesus Christ according to prophecy. Bible Prophecy deals with Jesus Christ as the Messiah of Israel reigning on earth (Matt. 19:28) over a kingdom promised to Israel in the Old Testament Scriptures. This is in fulfillment of the covenants of promise (Rom. 9:4; Eph. 2:12) that God made with that nation. There is a twofold purpose of God that is revealed in the Epistle of Colossians Chapter 1:15 – 20. Everything in Heaven and in Earth was created by Christ and for Him. However, both are in the hands of a usurper today. What we find in the New Testament is a plan whereby God will reconcile both realms back to himself by means of the redeeming work of Calvary. Two different programs are involved (Prophecy and the Mystery). Two different elect agencies are involved (Israel and the church the Body of Christ). Two different eternal destinies are involved -- a Heavenly for the Body of Christ (2Cor. 5:1; 1Cor. 15:51; 1Thess, 4:17) and an Earthly for Israel (Rev. 5:10). The end result is that in all things Jesus Christ will be preeminent. .

The New Testament Scripture–Rightly Divided

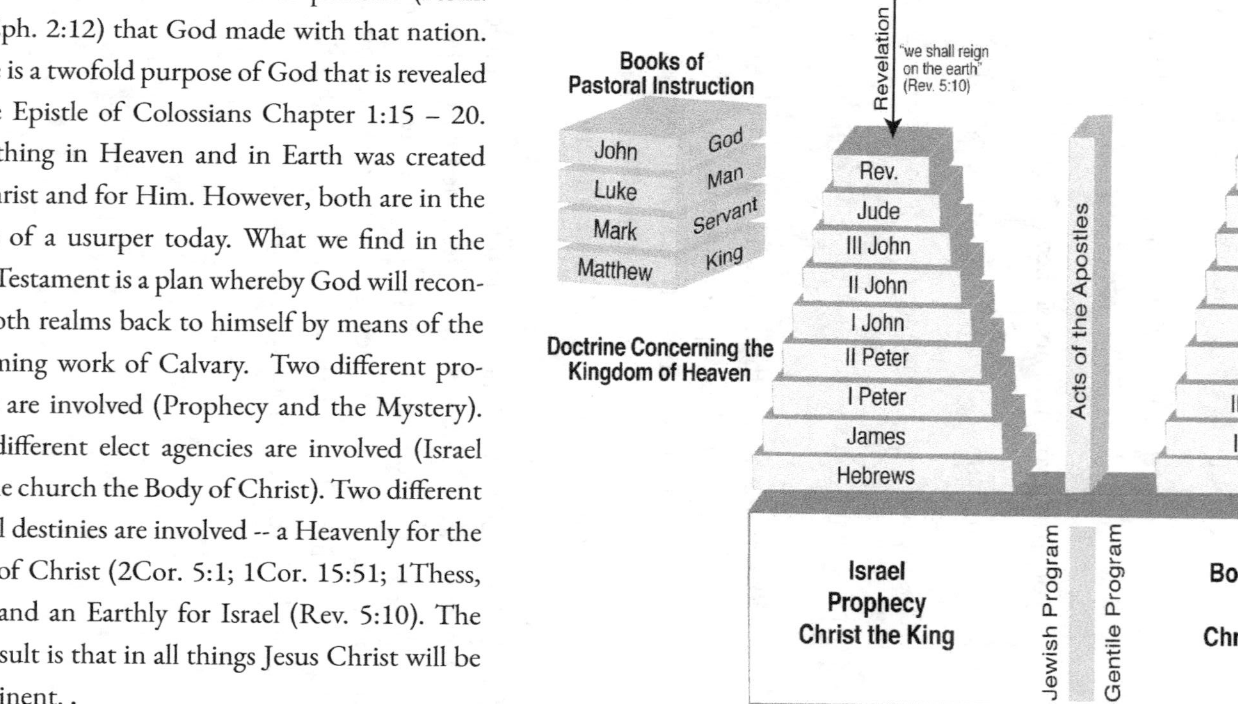

	Prophecy	The Mystery
Purpose	That Christ might reign over the earth [Jer. 22:15; Zech. 9:9-12]	That in all things, Christ might be preeminent [Col 1:18]
Goal	A kingdom established on this earth [Jer. 23:5]	A body given a position in heaven [Eph 1:19-23; 2:5-6; Col 3:1-3; II Cor. 5:1]
Elect Agency	Redeemed Israel (Ex 19:5; Deut 14:2) / A Holy Nation, a Royal Priesthood (1 Pet 2:9)	The Church which is His Body (Col 1:18, 24)
Relation to Christ	Christ as it's King [Isa. 9:6-7]	Christ as its Head [Eph. 1:19-23; 5:23]
Relation of Jews to Gentiles	Israel Supreme [Isa. 60:10-12; 61:6]	Jew & Gentile on the same level [Rom. 10:12; 11:32; Eph. 2:15-17]
Blessings to the Gentiles	Through Israel [Isa. 60:1-3; Zech.8:23]	Independent of Israel [Act 28:27-28; Rom 11:11-15]
View of Nations	Mainly concerns nations [Isa. 2:4; Eze 37:21-22]	Concerned with individuals [Rom 10:12-13; II Cor. 5:14-17]
Nature of Blessings to Men	Blessings both material and spiritual on earth [Isa. 2;3; 11:1-9]	All spiritual blessings in heavenly places [Eph. 1:3; Col. 3:1-3]
View of the Lord's Presence	Concerns Christ's presence on earth [Isa. 59:20; Zech. 14:4]	Explains Christ's present absence from the earth [Eph. 1:20-23]
Means of Justification	Works must accompany faith [James 2:14-20; Mark 16:16]	Through faith alone [Rom. 3:21-26; 4:5; Eph. 2:8-9]
Relation to the Law of Moses	The Law of Moses in force [Mat. 28:20; cf. 23:2; Acts 23:20]	Law of Moses taken out of the way [Eph. 2:15; Col. 2:14]
Structure	Concerns a political organization [Dan. 2:44; Mat 6:10]	Concerns a body; a living organism [I Cor. 12:13; Eph 4:15]
Miraculous Sign - Gifts	Required as evidence of faith [Mark 16:17]	Done away; replaced by unfeigned love (charity) [I Cor. 13:8]
Apostleship	The twelve apostles, 12 thrones, 12 tribes [Mat. 19:28]	Paul [Rom. 11:13; Eph. 2]
Commission	Preach & baptize [Mat. 28:19; Mark 16:16]	Preach without baptism [I Cor. 1:17; I Cor. 12:13; cf. Eph. 4:5]
View of Christ's Return	Return to the earth to reign [Acts 1:11; cf. 2:36]	Return to the air (rapture) [I Thess. 4:17]

ABOUT THE AUTHOR

Michael J. Tiry came to know the Lord Jesus Christ as his personal Savior at the age of twenty-nine while in the midst of a career as an engineer. Michael served in the United States Civil Service as a professional engineer for 25 years. After 25 years with the civil service, Michael also started, owned and operated a private engineering company. While engaged in a career as an engineer, he also was involved with other men in the founding a local Bible believing church. His deep appreciation for having the assurance of eternal life, his passion for study, and his quest for truth compelled him to search deeply into the Bible with a desire to learn its truth that he might present the riches of God's grace to others. Over the last forty five plus years Michael has been involved in itinerant preaching, a church planting ministry, and a teaching and preaching ministry at Berean Bible Church in Chippewa Falls, Wisconsin. Michael also serves Berean Bible Church as director of the Timothy Institute – a Bible curriculum designed to prepare men for leadership in local churches. Additionally, Mike has been active over a span of twenty three years in a prison ministry. Michael and his wife Lin.

www.ingramcontent.com/pod-product-compliance
Lightning Source LLC
Chambersburg PA
CBHW081927120726

47997CB00010B/3073